TWO
FISH
ON ONE
HOOK

TWO
FISH
ON ONE
HOOK

A Transformative Reading
of Thoreau's *Walden*

Raymond P. Tripp, Jr.

△ LINDISFARNE BOOKS

Published by Lindisfarne Books
3390 Route 9, Hudson, NY 12534

Library of Congress Cataloging-in-Publication Data

Tripp, Raymond P. (Raymond Plummer), 1932–
    Two Fish on one hook : a transformative reading of
    Thoreau's Walden / Raymond P. Tripp, Jr.
       p. cm.
    ISBN 0-940262-89-4 (pbk.)
    1. Thoreau, Henry David, 1817–1862. Walden.
    2. Thoreau, Henry David, 1817–1862–Technique.
    3. Reader-response criticism. 4. Literary form. I. Title.
    PS3048.T69 1998
    818'.303–dc21   98-40547
                                          CIP

10 9 8 7 6 5 4 3 2 1

Printed in the United States of America

CONTENTS

Still — for Susan

1
PROLEGOMENON

People read *Walden* because it is an important book. They write books about it, because like Thoreau they "dearly love to talk," and also because "the echo is, to some extent, an original sound, and therein is the magic and charm of it." The ideal reader of *Walden* becomes a co-author. But as important as *Walden* is, it is becoming less well understood and more subtly misrepresented as the present century comes to a close.

All this would be little to worry about if *Walden* were not one of a select number of "true books." But many people hunger for a book "which will explain [their] miracles and reveal new ones," only to find themselves turned away when they look up and are misfed by the people who control how Thoreau is served. No doubt we can worry too much about the fate of *Walden* and what it says, since, as its primary author reminds us, "We may waive just so much care of ourselves as we honestly bestow elsewhere." But every day there is greater likelihood that people who admire *Walden* will be seriously misinformed when like "some ill-fed village hound yielding to the instinct of the chase" they turn to other books to learn more about Thoreau and find themselves turned against him.

With precious few exceptions, a trip to a library or to a bookseller will turn up volumes written by the very kind of desperate people Thoreau is talking about: materialists of one stripe or another, who in their ignorance, vanity, or silly animosity toward transcendentalism do their misguided best to debunk the man and his masterpiece with unworthy explanations. The chances of finding a book which takes Thoreau at *his* word are very slim. A few books do, of course, reject the recently re-imaged, dark, young, queer Thoreau, but, as he himself would say, even these too often remain "commonly courtier-like" in bowing to "scholar-like thoughts." At their best, books about *Walden* and its author seem partial, in some ways insightful, but unevenly so. And more often than not, unless we live near a large library, such studies are hard to get hold of and, even then, not always easy to identify. For these reasons, there is need for a transcendental reading of Thoreau's transcendental book.

As urgent as this need may be, filling it is not easy. Co-authoring a book about *Walden* is truly "a labor to task the faculties of a man." Since Thoreau as the saying goes is the real thing, anyone who attempts a book about his book, as echoic as the effort must be, learns right away that the critic too must write "a simple and sincere account of his own life." A book about a book must also be something of an original source in its own right, even though it is obvious from the start that people who write about *Walden* "may be sure that they have been anticipated." Difficulties aside, there is nonetheless reason to try, because time passes, people change, language needs up-dating, and truth is never unimportant.

Thoreau opens and closes his argument on a communicative note. He opens it with "I would fain say something," and closes it with "I desire to speak somewhere *without* bounds; like a man in a waking moment, to men in their waking moments." Throughout *Walden* he struggles against his own suspicion that the most important things "are never communicated by man to man." What he has to say and the way he says it, however, come very close to being the same thing, like a noun and a verb from the same root; and this unity of end and means defines his rare achievement. For this reason alone it is most important to heed the way he has put his book together, as he tries to say more of the unsayable, so that (like Emily Dickinson) instead of getting to heaven at last, he and his reader are going all along. We must, in a word, follow the pattern Thoreau sets up in *Walden* and approach his work as *an act of communication.*

Contrary to what many people think, the truths that Thoreau communicates never fully disappear from the world. As obscure as his "cheering information" may seem, "the at present unutterable things we may find somewhere uttered." Even in dark centuries like Thoreau's nineteenth, and our darker twentieth, the truth of human nature and destiny is always somewhere to be found. Wise souls like Thoreau incarnate and devote their lives to restating perennial truths in words their contemporaries may better understand. And as a result, although the ageless truths in *Walden* have been repeated in every age, not until Thoreau rephrases them in order to correct the old errors into which the New World was again falling, are they pronounced with such nasal ferocity and Yankee wit. In this immemorial effort he joins illustrious company, like his older Danish and Scottish contemporaries Søren Kierkegaard and Thomas Carlyle, his neighbor Emerson, and his younger Amherst colleague Emily Dickinson.

Thoreau's position in the spiritual history of the West holds a special interest for people who have read other "true books." Such readers discover that they have a number of good friends in common with Thoreau, and they are happy to rejoin some of them in *Walden* and, as Thoreau says in "Visitors," even "with their bodies." Thoreau's position in the high society of the mind speaks not only to the centrality of his thinking and the breadth of its basis in tradition but also to the depth and significance of his book as the instrument of his ideas. We do not need to pursue these other voices, in order to read *Walden* well, for "God will see that you do not want society," and readers will hear many "cheering visitors" conversing in the Concord woods, where "a quiet mind may ... have as cheering thoughts, as in a palace." The right book will come along at the right time. In any case, there is no better source of "cheering information" than mixing with great minds across continents and centuries.

The best strategy, therefore, for reading and writing about *Walden* is to do what Thoreau does: to follow the patterns he sets up and to approach his work as *an act of communication*—that is, to listen, to hear, and to act upon what he has to say. Admittedly, this can be hard going at first, for *Walden* opens on what seems to many to be a stern and uncharitable note. Since it makes no sense to talk at people whose heads are full of nonsense, the first thing Thoreau has to do is to remove all conceptual tomfoolery—and that he does. Consequently, his first chapter sets unceremoniously about to relieve us of what we do not need and to remind us of what we do not know. Even though this may seem an uncharitable way to begin, as Thoreau wryly suggests, "You must have a genius for charity as well as for anything else." Since opposition is true friendship, he always insists on clearing the air, and our brains, so that we all know exactly where we stand or fall. Like it or lump it, this is the way Thoreau writes, *Walden* reads, and the truth works.

Neither Thoreau nor his book is in any way sentimental. It is an understatement to say that his opening theme is less than diplomatic. When he writes, "How can he remember well his ignorance—which his growth requires—who has so often to use his knowledge," his *he* is *us*. Thoreau dwells on this point: "To know that we know what we know, and that we do not know what we do not know, that is true knowledge." If the hat fits, we are told to wear it. As reluctant as we may be to face up to the fact that our knowledge may be ignorance, we are admonished to "try our lives by a thousand simple tests." And Thoreau includes himself, confessing that "If I had remembered this it would have prevented some mistakes." Spiritual as well as physical aches and pains need to be diagnosed before they can be treated and cured. At the very least, an author who reminds us that there is no "safety in stupidity alone" and then, looking over our shoulder while we are reading his book, does not omit to tell us, "It is not all books that are as dull as their readers"—such an author cannot be charged with elevating courtesy into a religion. Thoreau is the last one to contract himself into "a nutshell of civility."

Accordingly, Thoreau's first step is to remind us of how very idle and blockheaded we are. The busy folk "mind[ing] their own affairs" he leaves to their own devices. Books about *Walden* are also obliged to begin on the right note by sounding Thoreau's stern wake-up call. Many will find it a jarring note, but there is no better way to wake from the Procrustean "sense of men asleep" and to get "a sick one to lay down his bed and run" into *Walden* in time. It may be wisdom to let the dead bury the dead; but Thoreau is convinced that "a man is not required to bury himself." He, therefore, begins by asking his readers "Why should they begin digging their graves as soon as they are born?"

2
GRACEFUL
COMMUNICATION

Trying to explain what *Walden* says is a bootstrap task, because it cannot be done without facing the same problems that Thoreau did in trying to communicate new ideas to people still thinking in "some derivative old-country mode." In approaching *Walden* as an attempt to say something or, more abstractly, as an act of communication, we have to reflect upon the difficulties of any revelation. For while we are discoursing upon the mysteries of communication, we must depend upon their operation. Specifically, when we try to make what is silent *audible* and what is invisible *visible* again, in the light of the day, there is no way but to stitch new word-skins for the wine which never ages.

Books about books, however, run the risk of running in circles and getting tangled in the seams of sartorial archeology, digging up and patching cultural hand-me-downs as they must. Thoreau himself jokes about the circularity of such "tailoring" in an allusion to his first effort at sewing new ideas in *A Week on the Concord and Merrimack Rivers*. This first attempt to reweave strands of the perennial tradition, he jokes, resulted in a "basket of a delicate texture" that did not sell. *Walden* is his second go at writing a marketable book "worth any one's while to buy." He compared the chapters in *A Week* to statues in a gallery, which, because they were not holding hands, were assumed to be unrelated. Thoreau set out to correct this situation in *Walden*, which only in the last of seven manuscript revisions was divided into chapters. Looking closely, therefore, at his communicative strategies is crucial to understanding how *Walden* actually works, for he had learned that the best art is not always invisible weaving.

Whether we read *Walden* as literature, philosophy, religion, or even autobiography, the key to understanding what Thoreau has to say lies in keeping an eye on his calculated use of language. If this is a truism, it is a neglected one. The number of surviving manuscripts show that it is no exaggeration to say that almost every word is handpicked seven times over. Needless to say, a good imagination also comes in very handy, since reading *Walden* in any way other than the way it was written won't get anyone very far. Thoreau learned that the first thing he had to do, since he could not water down the truth, was to buoy up the reader. He had to provide the literary equivalent of what theologians call grace, giving his readers not only the hard facts but also the ability to read them. Someone must give if the basket is to change hands. Thoreau decided to educate the buyer: "Yet not the less, in my case, did I think it worth my while to weave them, and instead of studying how to make it worth men's while to buy my baskets, I studied rather how to avoid the necessity of selling them."

Avoid is the key word in this refinement of Emerson's legendary "mousetrap" market theory, for real communication obviates the need. In other words, creating an honest demand for the real thing gets rid of the need for the rhetorical hard sell which speaks down to the reader. This is another way of describing the essential problem Thoreau sets about solving.

Just the same, it is not surprising that some readers question Thoreau's success in overcoming the difference "between the speaker's meaning and the lexical meaning" of the language he uses. Many still see *Walden* as a collection of woodsy, sometimes clever, sometimes confessional, but at best loosely related essays written in the manner of the seventeenth-century writer Thomas Browne, whom Thoreau admired. They would not let Thoreau out of the woods and forget that he tells us he left them "for as good a reason as I went there," because "I had several more lives to live." Nowadays the safe picture of Thoreau the man of nature who penned rambling essays about the woods is seldom stated in so many words, but it survives in the assumption that Thoreau's book is a transcendental Humpty-Dumpty that needs to be put back together again. All kinds of academic glue are applied to the job of re-imaging the dark, young, queer Thoreau, who got bogged down in counting seeds, and recording unscientific data. But the application of aesthetics, biology, linguistics, politics, or psychology is confused and doesn't hold. No apology is needed. Drawing upon disciplines which are an expression of the naive materialism Thoreau is trying to dispel is contradictory and mischievous, because the flywheels, belts, and pulleys of outdated science deny what *Walden* is all about. Academic engineering can never show how transcendental gears actually mesh. The teeth in Thoreau's communicative machinery are made of his mythological virtuosity and driven by his metaphysics.

But metaphysical virtuosity can become a literary vice. Thoreau is fully capable of writing prose too good for his own good. Shelf after shelf of conflicting interpretations of *Walden* show this to be the case. Volumes of contradictory *readings*—as they are called—fill our libraries. These are not a sign that Thoreau failed to get his message across but that his readers failed to follow his signs. So tasty are his natural tonics for the ailing soul that great doses are often swallowed for the wrong reasons. "God's Drop" and "the pill which will keep us well, serene, [and] contented" are taken by the handful, like so many existential tranquilizers. If people who go to the doctor are notorious for not following his orders, people who read *Walden* are demonstrably worse for not following the author's instructions. Readers must guard against admiring Thoreau's art but missing his message. It is all too easy to lick the sugar coating off and to spit out the pill of truth. Spiritual doctors, "hunters as well as fishers of men" like Thoreau, frequently learn that their game relish the bait "without finding the skewer" and "know nothing about the hook of hooks with which to angle for" the health of their souls.

Although Thoreau understands communication inclusively, as something which encompasses all experience, including art, he is quick to condemn the abuse of art, including the abuse of his own. As we should expect, he is impatient with readers who reduce art to a palliative or a remedy for ordinary boredom: "The best works of art are the expression of man's struggle to free himself from his condition, but the effect of our art is merely to make this low state comfortable and that higher state to be forgotten." Today, Thoreau's words would apply not just to literary art but to other fields as well, such as psychiatry, where too often being "cured" means adjusting to what Thoreau calls "low condition" of being normal. Thoreau is not keen on catering to the appetites of normal readers. He agrees completely with Samuel Johnson that "consolation" and "comfort" can make "a prisoner ... patient under the inconveniences of confinement" but cannot set him free.

As *Walden* moves toward its own "Conclusion," Thoreau combines art and communication. In particular, his art communicates through an allegory of the seasons. The completion of his house parallels the completion of the year. As he plasters the walls of his house, the "temple, called his body," winter skims the pond with ice. Alluding to his own book with deep and organic punning, he likens

15

the "first ice" to the aesthetic surface of experience, upon which "you can *lie* [emphasis added] at your length," even if it is only an "inch thick," like his book. Good art can teach, but bad art can misinform and for a long time. But the clever person sees that such icing also "affords the best opportunity ... for examining the bottom where it is shallow." Good art and good books like the book *Walden* let us see through things.

The chilly skin of the natural world is only an "inch thick," but Thoreau tells us that when art is on the level, it can be indispensably useful as well as beautiful. We catch more of his allegory when he tells us that only a few days later "The beauty of the ice was gone, and it was too late to study the bottom." The "real beauty of something," in this case the usefulness of the ice on the pond, may not lie in the thing itself at all, but in something else we can see through to, and this second thing may lie in another direction altogether. Usable beauty is very short-lived and implies a duty—in this case, that we must make hay while the sun shines but before our opportunities melt away. In sum, art communicates in spite of its relative brevity and thinness, since like an ancient manuscript it lets us see through the hide side of things, including words.

Carrying "grace" back to the ability to read, Thoreau forges his communicative circle. The weak link in the chain lies, again, between "new" ideas and the "old-country mode" of thinking. For "to carve and paint the very atmosphere and medium through which we look" is the most private yet universal of arts. "We are all sculptors and painters, and our material is our own flesh and blood and bones," and the results are predictably uneven, enough to make even Thoreau "despair of getting anything quite simple and honest done in this world with the help of men." But who is to say? "Could a greater miracle take place than for us to look through each other's eyes for an instant?"

There is always more to the art of nature and to the art of reading books like *Walden* than some readers dream of. "The amount of it is, the imagination, give it the least license, dives deeper and soars higher than Nature goes." Throughout *Walden* Thoreau's stress upon the personal tragedy of the wasted meaning and lost power within our trivialized lives supplies another facet of his protean imagery. None of us can "kill time without injuring eternity."

Because Thoreau's message is about much more than sticks and stones, he faces a problem which goes beyond writing clearly. According to Owen Barfield, any writer who engages more than the empirical world "is under a double obligation." It is not enough then to argue faultlessly for heterodox ideas. A reasonable writer must also try to account for the erroneous opinions of the orthodox majority.

When these opinions spell materialism, there is need to make a number of important distinctions. It is necessary, for example, to clarify the difference between what is *subtle* and what is merely *complex*. Maintaining this distinction requires Thoreau to deal with qualities as well as quantities. Since *Walden* moves from natural forms to seamless ideas, Thoreau must deal with matters of kind as well as degree. There is a risk that what is merely complicated or ambiguous may displace what is subtle and ineffable. Difficulties in language, of course, can spring from many a quarter, but here in particular they are likely to crop up in the difference between grasping one idea well and juggling many. When Thoreau warns us that *Walden* has no "visible inlet or outlet except by the clouds," he is saying that transcendental logic does not turn on ordinary syllogistic gears but proceeds from subtlety to subtlety. It is not a matter of moving parts but of sequential refinement, whereas complexity is merely multiplied opacity. Because Thoreau aims at nothing less than communicating higher truths, nothing less than a complementary effort on the reader's part will do.

Without rigor the confusion of qualities and quantities, subtleties and complexities, and so forth, leads back into the very relativism *Walden* aims to dispel. As if Thoreau does not trust his own words, he speaks with two voices. Often after developing an idea figuratively, to help us out, he will stop and speak directly. To make sure that we realize he has "never assisted the sun *materially* [emphasis added] in his rising," he will remind us in so many words that every fact has a higher and lower meaning.

If for a moment we forget this communicative leap between the two poles of Thoreau's art, we are sure to miss the cast of his thought and catch very little of the life in and around Walden, the book or the pond, where things are not always what they seem to be, but peculiarly double and otherwise. It is two fish on one hook, birds under water, fish in the sky, lost dogs and discovered selves, feathery warmth in icy snow, "demoniac laughter" of divine loons, or green weeds under winter ice, and so on, until at last we catch on to the fact that reading this one book requires two authors hooked on the steely barb of truth. Thoreau, helpful as usual, does not fail to tell us so:

> The cars never pause to look at it; yet I fancy that the engineers and firemen and brakemen, and those passengers who have a season ticket and see it often, are better men for the sight. The engineer does not forget at night, or his nature does not, that he has beheld this vision of serenity and purity once at least during the day.

Likewise, we as readers, with our seventy or so season tickets, will see more than we ever suspected as we ride our minds through Walden, book or pond. In the night of death when our life pass has expired, our souls at least will be the better for our having lived and read—than never having read at all.

As this parable also shows, Thoreau constructs *Walden* so that its literal level always invites allegorizing. In another parable (which glances again at the failure of *A Week*), he tells us how "one of those great cakes" of Walden ice, representing *Walden* the book, "slips from the ice-man's sled into the village street, and lies there for *a week* [emphasis added] like a great emerald, an object of interest to all passers." Where we might expect "passers-*by*," Thoreau omits the prepositional ending "-by," to achieve the simpler and less common form "passers." By doing this he brings other meanings of the verb "to pass" into play. These suggest that he expects many readers to take a look, and "to *pass*," that is, "not to partake," with a polite no thank you. The first person center of Thoreau's allegorizing connects everything he writes *in* his book *to* his book, himself, and to ourselves as readers. The result is a transparent overlay of biographical, literary, philosophical, and religious levels of meaning. As we read, *Walden* the book is forever rising and disappearing into its higher meanings. "Ice," he reminds us in passing, "is an interesting subject for contemplation." Ice evaporates and seeks its "volatile truth," while Thoreau's book soars into its "higher and more ethereal life." Not infrequently we are obliged to lower our eyes to the solid edges of the actual book in our hands, which "full of light and reflections, becomes a lower heaven itself so much the more important."

"No visible inlet or outlet" translates into the absence of an academic escalator or, as Jonathan Swift said, a mechanical operation of the spirit, to carry the lazy reader into Concord. Thoreau in his often-quoted recipe for reading puns on de*liber*ately. We are to get in and out of *Walden* by reading un*book*ishly, so that we can see the forest for the trees in "Life in the Woods." His directions are explicit: "To read well, that is, to read true books in a true spirit, is a noble exercise, and one that will task the reader more than any exercise which the customs of the day esteem…. How many a man has dated a new era in his life from the reading of a book!"

Walden, moreover, is a special kind of "true book," a report, and it reports an experience vital to all of us. A personal urgency organizes Thoreau's varied acts of communication and immediately separates *Walden* from the great mass of books that are *not* gospel. Writing scripture places the greatest responsibility upon an author, since any book of cosmic journalism must be more than ordinarily clear, as we have seen, and capable of turning the mind, so we can hear news from heaven as well as history from hell.

Thoreau's labors are remarkable not only for their larger strategies but also for an immense and thematic richness of images. His numerous references to wakefulness are typical. "It is," he slyly admonishes his reader, "after all, always the first person that is speaking" and the second person listening—the first Person being the Divine Person. Readers inevitably speak with themselves, so that they may learn to recognize the voice of the "spectator … that is no more I than it is you" behind their own voices. Thoreau's relentless wake-up call, however, is not just rhetoric; he means exactly what he says: "I would fain say something, not so much concerning the Chinese and Sandwich Islanders as you who read these pages, who are said to live in New England; something about your condition." This is hardly the language of objective science, written and read by nobody. Nor is this the language of the psychological *I*, sitting out a half-life of suspended disbelief and slowly turning into lead.

Thoreau's language rules out second-rate science, as C. S. Lewis writes, where "The Subject is as empty as the Object," and "almost nobody has been making linguistic mistakes about almost nothing." On the contrary, his language rather suspends belief in the modern view of things. His audience is "said to live in New England," but it is hard to say just where in the ancient geography of their own limitations they do live, or if they are really alive or merely dead on their feet as they were in Old England. In *Walden* no "as if" is allowed. The *I* is ultimately the best, eternal part of Thoreau; and the *you* is you his actual reader in "your [present] condition." If something more than this present *you* wakes in us, should we complain?

Punning on "hear" and "add up," Thoreau complains, "My accounts ... I have, indeed, never got *audited* [emphasis added]." He invites the world to audit his accounts in the cosmic trade. *Walden* is an open invitation—even a challenge—to check his numbers as these are reported in his figures. A large share of his imaginative capital is expended in issuing the psychological prospectus of his enterprise, and he is willing to underwrite his readers' literal liabilities, to provide seed money, and even to guarantee out-of-pocket costs. Yet in spite of his invitation, he does not flatter us with the expectation that we will all invest well and received huge dividends, for he tells us "I have not set my heart on that."

Thoreau knows full well that poor mental economy leads to an emotional deficit and a reluctance on the part of readers not to become "passers" but to stop and look, to see if this new emerald basket called *Walden* holds water. Names for these mental debits can be culled from a number of disciplines. Complementary lists of words may be arranged on either side of the philosophical ledger. On one side we find: *objective, rational, discursive, material, secular, modern,* and so on; and on the one side: *subjective, intuitive, immediate, spiritual, religious, perennial,* and so on. But regardless of the terminology we may prefer to use in describing the desperate doubleness of our own condition, the practical problem of saying something new remains the same. Thoreau must overcome the mental recession which inhibits our consumption—and thus the circulation—of his ideas.

21

We can see, when talk about communication begins, how easy it is to get carried away by "the magic and charm of it." Reasonably enough, in marketing his basket of delicate texture, Thoreau tries to break down our sales resistance, through many other figures besides *waking up*. He also speaks in an idiom of *space*, which he equates with a state of mind and uses as another weapon against our collective hard-headedness. Thoreau is convinced that "we know not where we are. Beside, we are sound asleep nearly half our time." Waking up, then, to where we are is the first step in finding our way home. But no matter what metaphor he chooses to use, through an extraordinary range of images, Thoreau presents the communication of new knowledge as a unique three-step *experience*, which, in requiring growth and change, goes far beyond the Hegelian machinery of thesis-antithesis-synthesis. He can, for example, use the language of hunting as he invites us to roam the sovereign woods of the mind in pursuit of "nobler game." If we keep pace, we too will discover that we have left Socrates and his intellectual descendants, such as Hegel, running in abstract circles forever "farther from the true end of life." Thoreau reminds us that our "head is hands and feet," "an organ for burrowing" into life: "To be a philosopher is not merely to have subtle thoughts, nor even to found a school, but so to love wisdom as to live according to its dictates, a life of simplicity, independence, magnanimity, and trust. It is to solve some of the problems of life, not only theoretically, but practically." He confirms the inadequacy of merely intellectual synthesis and the need for hands-on analysis in a parable about making bread where, he says, "my discoveries were not by the synthetic but analytic process." But, as always in Thoreau, first comes the hard part, "the hard bottom and rocks in place."

We have to let our ignorance hit the ground and go to pieces on the stones at the bottom of the mind. First, we must see limited knowledge for the ignorance it can become, then we must admit new knowledge, and only after that can we put our Humpty-Dumpty lives back together again. A theologian might call such realignment of the mind by the Greek word *metanoia*, "turning of the mind" or repentance. Thoreau does not, because words as words are important only insofar as they help, as religious talk is nowadays not very likely to do. But in any case remaining a materialist is out of the question. No fudging or blurring whatsoever will do! Kicking stones is out! On the other hand *never* was an answer to *Who told you you were naked?* The legerdemain of old Adam always drops the ball. Thoreau is more than adamant: modern urbanites need not apply— not until they change their ways.

In *Walden* there is never any *privatio scientiæ*. Ignorance is never just an absence of knowledge, but an aggressive wrongheadedness parading as knowledge, and thereby displacing wisdom and ruling out new knowledge. A real effort must be made toward changing one's life. Would-be philosophers are admonished that "they should not *play* life, or *study* it merely, while the community supports them at this expensive game, but earnestly *live* it from beginning to end." Otherwise, nothing can happen except the "common dilettantism" of perpetual fun and games. Thoreau is not communicating death, but life. He is not a Socratic comedian.

Indeed, such knowledge as Thoreau would transmit changes communication into that encompassing learning for—after—life which Christians call salvation and Emerson called "the formation of the soul." Thoreau's knowledge is much more than the homogenized benevolence of gradually getting to be a better person. There are necessary steps along the way that translate learning into graduated maturation. The thinker who would catch holy ghosts in cages can never net the culprit called life. The earth on which we dwell is itself "but *dry land*," and there is no fixed point of lever-age, Archimedean or otherwise, with which to dislodge ig-norance. We have to get our heads busy, which is to say, our feet wet and hands dirty. Again, we have to follow Thoreau when he reports how he mines the truth from books: "Time is but the stream I go a-fishing in…. My head is hands and feet. I feel all my best faculties concentrated in it. My in-stinct tells me that my head is an organ for burrowing, as some creatures use their snout and fore paws, and with it I would mine and burrow my way through these hills."

Thoreau built his cabin with secondhand boards, old nails, and a borrowed axe. He built *Walden* with ideas for nails and borrowed books for boards, and we readers must do the same. To begin our "burrowing…through these hills," we too must borrow not an axe and boards but Tho-reau's words. To work our way into his book we must also presume that language communicates well enough to let us use our own season tickets, cross under and over, and graze in *Walden*'s amazing pastures, where there is room enough for the imagination. An awareness of personal impedi-ments comes first, then comes the knowledge that over-comes sleep and abstraction, for "To be awake is to be alive." Then we will no longer be "overcome with drowsi-ness," but "awake enough for…a poetic or divine life." Thoreau's concluding image of waking—"The sun is but a morning star"—puns on "son" and "sun." His echoing of Revelation 22:16, "I am the root and the offspring of David, and the bright and morning star," confirms that in adding *Walden* to the "Scriptures of the nations" he too is playing the daring game of revelation.

3

AS ABOVE, SO BELOW

As surprising as it may seem, *Walden* is organized according to the ancient Hermetic principle: *As above, so below*. While Thoreau's concluding image, "The sun is but a morning star," points to his scriptural intentions, it also points to this structural principle. *As above, so below* epitomizes the architecture of his book, which is organized according to a logic of progressive refinement. Even Christ the "son" is *but* a "morning star" compared to the Sun Father.

As above, so below shapes the language to and from *Walden*, sometimes in single phrases such as "spring of springs," and at other times at greater length, as in "The phenomena of the year take place every day in a pond on a small scale…. The day is an epitome of the year." *Walden* is full of implied comparisons like "sky water," "open a window under my feet," "Every child begins the world again," "Morning brings back the heroic ages," "in the history of the individual, as of the race," or in "the reflected as well as the heavenly sun." In each case an architectonic harmony links a fact of the "understanding" to "a fact of the imagination." Occasionally the link is moral: "As I stand over the insect crawling amid the pine needles on the forest floor, … I am reminded of the greater Benefactor and Intelligence that stands over me the human insect." More often the point turns on the mind and perception: "The surface of the earth is soft and impressionable by the feet of men; and so with the paths which the mind travels." "We shall, perhaps, look down thus on the surface of the air at length, and mark where a still subtler spirit sweeps over it."

The active aspect of this *as above, so below* structure generates the threefold progression governing Thoreau's language. The movement from one level to another controls syntactical and stylistic features of all proportions. Words, phrases, sentences, paragraphs, entire chapters, and groups of chapters all display the same negative, positive, integrative progression toward ethereal realms. To those who miss this movement *Walden* will read like a briar patch of contrast and unresolved contradiction. Readers not in the habit of following his directions miss his penchant for hierarchy and homological comparison and, therefore, accuse him of a Chestertonian love of paradox. They do not listen long enough to hear how lower oppositions wheel around and resolve themselves into higher unities. The transcendental machinery of Thoreau's style is a subject in itself, but this particular reader attention deficit needs a closer look.

To say, for example, that if we "repent of anything," it should be our "good behavior" sounds paradoxical enough. But if we continue to listen, we will hear that *good* means the wisdom of the world, which we all know is foolishness. In a word, *good* in the worldly sense means *bad* in the transcendental. The sense of contradiction is generated by stopping too soon and failing to see how the structure of Thoreau's sentences actually works. In this way, levelheaded readers depress the movement of Thoreau's language into academic circles. But "in sane moment we regard only the facts, the case that is," which recalls Alexander Pope's famous observation that "All Discord, Harmony, not understood." Thoreau's constant breaking of lower laws in order to follow higher laws is far less of a stylistic vice than a therapeutic *de*vice, to make room for knowledge by displacing ignorance.

Reflecting this aggressive and properly revolutionary movement of thought, *Walden*'s eighteen chapters are organized into three major groups, each comprised of six chapters,[1] which for convenience may be numbered:

Chapters 1–6, "Economy" to "Visitors"
Chapters 7–12, "The Bean-Field" to "Brute Neighbors"
Chapters 13–18, "House Warming" to "Conclusion."

Each of these three larger groups performs a specific function in the book's overall plan, corresponding respectively to the three stages of Thoreau's message. The smaller movement between the chapters within these major sections in turn exhibits the same progression of meaning, function, and complementary structure, as does, again, the movement of thought within each chapter. Even the word choices that drive Thoreau's sentences work in the same way. At the outset, however, his syntactical virtuosity should not be allowed to obscure the larger structures of his book. For now it is enough to observe that even in its phrasing, *Walden*'s argument and structure are one and the same. On all levels, Thoreau's language and thought become the working equivalent of the "lower heaven" which nature is because it is there in front of us. *Walden* "constantly and obediently answers to our conceptions" and is even more convenient than nature, because we can carry it around in our hand. Tracing the connections among the first six chapters, however, must come first. With this in hand, the basic structure of the book can guide the reading of the remaining chapters. A sketch of the progression from

---

1. Those familiar with Eastern thinking will recognize the similarities between the organization of *Walden* and the three qualities (*gunas*) of matter (*prakriti*): "black" inertia or existential friction (*tamas*), "red" activity (*rajas*), and "white" balance and harmony (*sattva*). People who are asleep are dominated by *tamas*.

"Economy" to "Visitors" will be enough to show how the book's larger equivalences work.

An overview will remind us that whatever appears negative in *Walden*'s first six chapters turns out to be positive from the point of the recovery that follows. Cleaning house, so to speak, makes room for new ideas and the facts they produce. In this regard, these six chapters serve primarily to rid us of everything that is not truly ourselves and, therefore, what we do not need for the task of living. Organized deprivation culminates in an insight that equips us to proceed to reading the book's second and central group of six chapters, from "The Bean-Field" to "Brute Neighbors." As this program of subtractive rectification begins, we stand as ordinary human beings "encumbered with stables never cleaned, and one hundred acres of land, tillage, mowing, pasture, and wood-lot." But at the end of this extraordinary process, "our lives are stripped" and we have nothing left— not even the clothes on our back—as we stand listening in solitude to the voice of the silence.

The process is as relentless as it is thorough. First, in "Economy," we are jolted out of our sleep by a complete rejection of past experience as, step by step, we are disburdened of our grosser ignorances. Our "seniors" are unlikely to tell us "anything to the purpose." We are disinherited of the "inherited encumbrances" which number the "factitious cares and superfluous coarse labors of life." Admonished for acquiring more than we need of almost everything, from food to furniture, we are next reminded of what the phrase *necessary of life* really means—namely, enough and no more food, shelter, and clothing than is necessary to maintain our "vital heat." Our first task, in a word, is to stay alive and well as simply as possible.

Such economy, of course, is right away perceived as niggardliness, and predictably it is countered with the self-serving rejoinder that "all this is very selfish." So much self-improvement, people say, is uncharitable, if not out-right antisocial. But Thoreau is ready for this philanthropical dodge and counters with another reminder that real charity starts and stays at home. With characteristically complex wordplay, he tells us to sit still, and not to "*go* about doing good," but rather to "*set* about being good [emphasis added]." As Thoreau brings his first and most aggressively negative chapter, "Economy," to a conclusion, he recovers the inescapable burden of being meek and poor in spirit with an appeal to a life "always flourishing" in freedom.

Now that the "grossest groceries" have been dispensed with, *Walden*'s second and significantly double chapter, "Where I Lived, and What I Lived For," proceeds with further and more subtly urgent probing. Thoreau now turns to our emotional, intellectual, and spiritual errors, as these are expressed in place and purpose. After we have learned *how* to maintain our vital heat, we need to know *where*, *when*, and *why*, and this is what Thoreau next takes up. However contradictory it may appear to move from the freedom which concludes "Economy" to the confinement which opens "Where I Lived," the opposition between the search for truth and the "site of a house" is quickly resolved by Thoreau's psychologizing of space and time. Place, purpose, and timing are re-defined according to the meanings they carry for living a spiritual life. As Thoreau tells us: "Though the view from my door was still more contracted, I did not feel crowded or confined in the least. There was pasture enough for my imagination." In other words Thoreau "travelled a good deal in Concord," because he universalizes "where."

Any "where" will do because in living a spiritual life all places are the same place. If we know what we are about, then the earth will in fact become "a lower heaven itself so much the more important," indeed, the only heaven where "God culminates in the present moment" and spiritual journeys can be made. There can be no better place, because "Olympus," the home of the Gods, "is but the outside of the earth everywhere." Responsive readers, thus, have so far learned two subtractive truths: to live simply and to stay right where we are, in order to "set about being good." This, we learn, is "to live deep and suck all the marrow out of life." Our job is not to improve the world, but to know it, and through knowing it, to improve both ourselves and the world. All we need to do is too stay put and get busy, since "the richest vein is somewhere hereabouts"—as close at hand as the nearest copy of *Walden*.

But moving on, *Walden*'s third chapter, "Reading," seems once more to follow (or not to follow as some think) in contradiction. Thoreau has already told us that "one generation abandons the enterprises of another like stranded vessels," and does so wisely. So we are justified in asking what has reading, which deals with the past, to do with living? If we recollect, however, where we now are, we will again see that this opposition is calculated and only apparent. "Reading" follows according to the polar logic of progressive refinement.

Having set aside ordinary material success in life, and suppressed the itch to run off on ego-trips disguised as philanthropy, we find ourselves taking the next natural step in the pursuit of perfection. We know what we ought to be doing and where we ought to be doing it—namely, to *be* good here rather than to *do* good there. And we begin by reading reports of other *good* lives as these are recorded in books.

Accordingly, Thoreau closes his second chapter, involved as it is with locating and defining what is worth living for in this best of all worlds, with an amazing, forward-looking passage in which he equates his *head* with his hands and feet. Thoreau, like his mysterious and playful loon, does "all the work with his webbed feet beneath." If like William Langland's Piers Plowman we are going to dig in "God's

half-acre" for the best treasure, which is truth, the most
appropriate organ for burrowing into those mounds of the
past called books is the *head*:

> The intellect is a cleaver; it discerns and rifts its way
> into the secrets of things. I do not wish to be any more
> busy with my hands than is necessary. My head is hands
> and feet ... an organ for burrowing ... through these
> hills ... the richest vein is somewhere hereabouts; so by
> the divining-rod and thin rising vapors I judge; and
> here I will begin to mine.

To *begin to mine* is of course to read; and we can see that
these cognate activities oblige us to follow Thoreau's example and to "work and wedge our feet downward through the
mud and slush of opinion." Each of us, like the loon, must
also swim about *Walden* and explore its depths, "doing all
the work with his webbed feet beneath." If a person "let his
mind descend into his body and redeem it," head, hands,
and feet become a single organ of the soul and join the
voice as "one articulation of Nature." As we read our way
through *Walden*'s first six chapters, on our way to becoming
co-authors, we can see that the list of subtractive truths is
growing. The purpose of living simply, staying in one place,
and getting to work is about to be identified as study.

It is tempting to interrupt an overview of *Walden*'s first six
chapters and to join Thoreau's loon for a swim, in order to
admire his web-footed artistry. But such pleasures must wait
their turn. For now, it is indulgence enough to recall that
Thoreau's transitions are always far-reaching *transformations*, as in the present case, where, in anticipation of his
subsequent "cultivation" of the "volatile truth," "thin rising
vapors" show him where to "begin to mine" with his "head."

After "Where I Lived, and What I Lived For," however,
the chapters "Reading," "Sounds," "Solitude," and "Visitors" follow in what has become a familiar pattern. Each

chapter refines its predecessor by encompassing it in another patterned movement from negation through affirmation and on into more subtle integration. Reading as such is but one step in a larger process. And reading itself is submitted to progressive refinement and quickly broken down. A negative elimination of what Thoreau identifies as "'Little Reading'" leads, through a discussion of language, to a positive and rather Arnoldian, affirmation of the classics, as "the noblest recorded thoughts of man." But, as we should expect in the polar progression of Thoreau's thought, even this best reading turns out to be not quite good enough. Even the classics turn out to be provincial! Upon this note, in *Walden*'s fourth chapter, "Sounds," the reader is next carried beyond words and metaphor, and into the very stuff of sound. The opening sentence of this is itself a classic instance of transcendental diction.

Here the negation, affirmation, and integration of remembering our ignorance rather than using our knowledge, "which growth requires," are restated in terms of languages: "But while we are confined to books, though the most select and classic, and read only particular written languages, which are themselves but dialects and provincial, we are in danger of forgetting the language which all things and events speak without metaphor, which alone is copious and standard." Just as the classics rightly displace little reading, as the next step, the "vibration of the universal lyre" displaces the classics. The rhythms of nature surpass the hexameters of Homer—but not for long. The sounds of nature communicate a rich lesson, but in the end even her voice is not enough, because the imagination "dives deeper and soars higher than Nature goes." So after we have learned to listen to the audible Logos speaking through croaking frogs, hooting owls, baying hounds, and rattling commerce, we learn in the next and fifth chapter, "Solitude," that we must turn our inner ear to the Voice of the

Silence. There—if solitude is a place—we are prepared to experience the truly spiritual society by meeting ourselves: "However intense my experience, I am conscious of the presence and criticism of a part of me, which, as it were, is not part of me, but spectator, sharing no experience, but taking note of it, and that is no more I than it is you." Now we have been brought before the eternal Spectator, who is ourselves. Living simply in one place has passed beyond reading, beyond language, and even beyond sound itself, so that our reading knowledge extends to silence.

After this cathartic progression, the social activity implied by the sixth and final chapter, "Visitors," would seem to offer even greater contrast to the "Solitude" preceding it. But, as before, the apparent contradiction is quickly resolved. And this time the turnaround involves more than the psychologizing of space and engages the nature of Thoreau's guests. Thoreau does ask "What sort of space is that which separates a man from his fellows and makes him solitary?" but he then raises a Pauline question by reminding us that sometimes the "souls" who visited him did come "with their bodies." At other times, we are led to infer, they did not. The ethereal direction of *Walden's* first five chapters, moreover, shows that these visitors are as much aspects of their author's own make-up as they are flesh and blood—or for that matter *astral*—Concordians. In this final chapter, lessons learned in the most austere solitude are transformed into a higher sociability, and *Walden's* first and negative phase concludes with a happy assembly of "honest pilgrims."

In tracing the general scheme that holds *Walden's* first six chapters together, this outline has, for the most part, stuck to the main path among "the paths which the mind travels," which along the way open into many specific turns and intellectual vistas. Diagrammatically, as we shall see, digging in the right place = reading the right books = hearing the right message, and so on. In anticipation of "Visitors," for example, "Solitude" concludes with the society of the Gods, so that an archetypal conviviality, immediately preceding and leading into "Visitors," prepares us to meet "Hebe, cup-bearer to Jupiter," a Goddess "who had the power of restoring gods and men to the vigor of youth." Following Thoreau on the crisscrossing paths that lead from chapter to chapter presupposes that we have some inkling of where the main path will take us, and that our progress has not been circular, but rather spiral, because transcendental travel is seldom horizontal. Thoreau peels away layer after layer of the cloying ignorances that comprise ordinary life, only to return his reader, via the "old book" as we recall, to a richer, more abundant life. Not till we are lost—in other words not till we have lost the world—do we begin to find ourselves, and to realize where we are and how infinite are our relations.

As Thoreau's readers and potential co-authors, we find ourselves robbed—with elegant but pointed humor—of all that we formerly thought we knew and accepted. Gone are our views on buying and selling, our urge to be forever on the move, our little reading, reading itself, sounds, ordinary society, only to have our world restored to us clean, new, and unthinkably larger. In sum, from "Economy" to "Visitors" we progress from life as usual, through living simply, staying put, seeking, reading, and listening, until we enter the silence of "the great ocean of solitude." There we meet the Spectator in ourselves and "set about being good" with the "finest sediment" settling in from "continents on the other side." Equipped with this fresh insight, we are then sent back to read the world and taste the solid stuff of "beans," which is to say, we are directed forward into *Walden*'s second group of chapters, for a second look at the world.

We are now to put this trimming of the mind to good use. Much of the flushing refreshment of *Walden*'s first six

34

chapters may well originate in nothing more than Thoreau's topic and the irresistible enthusiasm with which he pursues it. But the actual instrument of his Olympian optimism and vigor is language. Thoreau's *words* are what work the communicative transformation that turns readers into co-authors. The harmonics of his thought informs words, weaves sentences, shapes paragraphs, and ties chapters together, and these verbal resonances enable us to join in the remarriage of heaven and earth at Walden Pond. "A lake like this is never smoother than at such a time; and the clear portion of the air above it being shallow and darkened by clouds, the water, full of light and reflections, becomes a lower heaven itself so much the more important."

In *Walden*, and other real places, it is always: *As above, so below.*

4

AND EVEN LOWER

Walden's first six chapters equip the reader with a transcendental point of view. The second group of six chapters then invites the reader to apply this insight to the world as "a kind of fiction, a work of the imagination only," but all the more important for that very reason. Before turning to the solid, time-bound stuff of the world as "The Bean-Field," however, we should look again at Thoreau's way of living and thinking and how it affects his writing on the most concrete level—word by word, sentence by sentence, and chapter by chapter. Thoreau may not approve of abstract "scholar-like thoughts," but he is uniquely precise and consistent. The choice of each word is as vital as the idea it carries. We cannot simply acknowledge that the *how* and *what* of his style are the same thing, and then continue to read as if this marriage of mind and language were unimportant. With Thoreau the style is indeed the man, and the man is the book.

A glance at the overall structure of *Walden* shows that every part, large and small, exists and works according to a pattern of negation, affirmation, and integration. The powerful presence of this pattern accounts for the two main ways Thoreau's book has been received. Viewed as a *function*, this pattern takes on the threefold character of a movement of thought. Viewed as a *structure*, it takes on the twofold character of a set of oppositions. Clearly, we tend to see what we look for, and this second, binary way of reading *Walden* accounts for Thoreau's reputed taste for contradiction and paradox.

Looking at the whole of *Walden*, then, we should expect to find these principles at work on a still grander scale. Thoreau's first and final chapters, "Economy" and "Conclusion," should, and do, exhibit the extreme poles of his style. "Economy" and "Conclusion" are at once the most powerfully complementary and the most vigorously opposed chapters in *Walden*. Specifically, "Economy" is the longest and most negative chapter of the first negative section, while "Conclusion" is almost the shortest but certainly the most positive of the third and most positive group of chapters. Together they enclose the substance of *Walden* within the most elegant working symmetry.

Sometimes, however, the very elegance of Thoreau's style seems to get in the way, and we get lost in the outrages and enchantments his words work upon us. But it is useful, as Thoreau says, to get "completely lost, or turned round," and it seems that he is keen that we do, so that we may "learn the points of the compass again." We may not otherwise be able to translate his formula of knowledge into experience. Instead of remembering our ignorance in order to learn, we might forget to get lost in order to find out where we are. Not until we take this step, as Thoreau reminds us, "do we appreciate the vastness and strangeness of nature.... Not till we are lost, in other words not till we have lost the world, do we begin to find ourselves." The bemusing ease of getting lost in Thoreau's woods, therefore, commands a scriptural purpose that goes with the territory. There is a risk that parts of *Walden* may be put out of mind because others are overprized, but it is a calculated risk Thoreau must take. Yet in the beginning, while Thoreau like St. John is completing a shorter version of his story, he is also setting, up word by word, the inner movement of thought which both leads and constitutes his message.

An overview of the dynamics of Thoreau's thought and the way it shapes all levels of the working structure of his book, should lead to an account of the ways his ideas specifically shape his phrases and sentences. Thoreau writes to convince, but he never condescends and writes down to his readers. He acknowledges that "there are more secrets" in his trade than in most others; but his refusal to hang "'No Admittance'" on the door of his cabin shows us that his intent is to reveal, rather than conceal, them. So, he seeks in explaining his explanation to accomplish this initiatory task and, in fact, devotes considerable space and time to it.

According to Thoreau's transcendental logic, our heads are too full of knowledge. As useful and not untrue as this old knowledge may be, it leaves little room for new knowledge. Therefore, if we are to escape the relative ignorance of our limited knowledge, we must *un*learn our certainties. As this is at once the problem and the formula for its solution, it is also the dynamic of Thoreau's style. To escape the opacity of our certainties, we need to know what these are, and it is the first business of *Walden* to tell us. Accordingly, from the outset, by speaking from a relentlessly transcendental point of view, Thoreau encourages us to reverse the ordinary, material way of looking at things and words. We would be hard put, for example, to find a more sweeping or more compact condemnation of the way things are than the sentence that wraps up Thoreau's opening paragraph: "At present I am a sojourner in civilized life again."

A look at this characteristic sentence will anticipate the way that working between two worlds shapes transcendental prose. Each word is at once concave, convex, and compound, because it functions in two graduated directions: upward to ethereal and downward to material meanings. In this way the light of Thoreau's language enters the labyrinth of our knowledge. Each word works like a lens, with one facet exposed to heaven and the other to earth, so that higher and lower worlds "glimmer on both its surfaces." The result is, as it were, a double focus that integrates our perceptions "not only theoretically, but practically." Each word is, therefore, also a vital boundary phenomenon, a verbal soul between the world and the mind, and comprises another *tertium quid*, or third thing, like grace. Dualized minds need words of this kind in order to connect visible objects with invisible meanings. Both Thoreau and his senior Emerson concur with Owen Barfield that metaphor finds an empirical basis in human consciousness:

> Men do not invent those mysterious relations between separate objects, and between objects and feelings or ideas, which is the function of poetry to reveal.... Connections between discrete phenomena, connections which are now apprehended as metaphor, were once perceived as immediate realities. As such the poet strives, by his own efforts, to see them, and to make others see them, again.

In transcendental language, through experience metaphor can resume its original literalness, as words reorient themselves according to new centers of being.

Applying this Janus principle to Thoreau's sentence, "At present I am a sojourner in civilized life again," we can see how its doubleness works. For each word and phrase there is both an empirical and a transcendental meaning. *At present*, for example, implies other times and places of equal or greater importance and a complementary dissatisfaction with here and now. *I am a sojourner* suggests that the speaker is a visitor, whose brief stay extends the disappointment, reinforces the otherness, and confirms the inadequacy of *civilized life*, which is neither the only nor even the best *life*. And *again* reverses as well as reinforces all that has gone before, reminding us that one visit may not be enough to master the plausibility of this world that induces belief. Thoreau's temporal style can communicate his *a*temporal message, because each word and phrase commands two referents.

Such concave-convex sentences like "At present I am a sojourner in civilized life again" are the rule rather than the exception in *Walden*. Understanding any one of them involves a big reading that integrates two points of view. Oppositions resolve into new unities as we move from structure to function. We have already glanced at the way logic and syntax reflect the homological principle *as above, so below*: "The greater part of what my neighbors call good I believe in my soul to be bad, and if I repent of anything, it is very likely to be my good behavior." Here again Thoreau is characteristically circumspect and sly. He does not condemn everything, only the *greater part*, which comparatively speaking makes the implied situation even worse. In this case, the shallow error implied by *call* is further condemned by the sincerity of *believe* and the depth of *soul*, while *if* and *very likely* suggest good reasons for not repenting. When we have followed the spiralling reversals and progressions of Thoreau's thought and arrived at the end of his sentence, we know very well that the *good behavior* of this world is nothing if not bad. Everything depends upon revising our estimate of *good* according to a transcendental point of view. We leave the sentence feeling that Thoreau is right in refusing to repent of this "lower heaven itself so much the more important."

In "Where I Lived, and What I Lived For" neighbors are the butt of another masterfully textured inversion of the "commonest sense," which is "the sense of men asleep": "I found myself suddenly neighbor to the birds; not having imprisoned one, but having caged myself near them." Once again, looking at the matter through the concave-convex lens of words, we can see that *found* and *suddenly* imply discovery and revelation. Throughout *Walden* Thoreau is concerned with the relativity of space, asking repeatedly who precisely are his neighbors, and "What sort of space is that which separates a man from his fellows and makes him solitary?" Anticipating the title of a later chapter "Brute Neighbors," here he presents himself as a brute *neighbor of the birds*, real ones with feathers, to be sure, but also heavenly ones. The verb phrases *not having imprisoned* and *but having caged* implicitly condemn business-as-usual in the penal colony of ordinary society, while at the same time they indicate that by confining the brute in himself, Thoreau avoids the old error of trying to possess heaven by trapping holy ghosts in institutional cages. In a similar vein, the pun in "my *with*drawing room [emphasis added]" from "Visitors" confirms the solitude transcendental society requires. As long as our drawing rooms are crowded, we are unlikely to hear from ourselves. A transcendental perspective reverses the language of incarceration.

Thoreau's two uses of the word *obscurity* offer perhaps the quintessential example of the way the polarities of his transcendental logic shape his style. In two passages that hearken back to the homological comparison between plaster and ice, we see him making communicative use of the fact that hard surfaces enable us to read what is behind them: "My house never pleased my eye so much after it was plastered.... Should not every apartment in which man dwells be lofty enough to create some *obscurity* [emphasis added] overhead, where flickering shadows may play at evening about the rafters?" Certainty about heaven never reaches very high. Later he once more turns to the paradoxical usefulness of opaque surfaces: "I do not suppose that I have attained to obscurity, but I should be proud if no more fatal fault were found with my pages on this score than was found with the Walden ice."

Thoreau's story of how one winter day he tossed his axe on the pond and lost it through a hole in the ice becomes a transcendental allegory. His reporting of how he "lay down on the ice and looked through the hole, until I saw the axe a little on one side, standing on its head" repeats the moral. Clearly, the pages of *Walden* cover Thoreau's thought just as the ice covers the pond. But in both cases surfaces enable us to use our head to see what lies beneath. And in *Walden*, where many things are reversed and "head is hands and feet," beneath is also overhead. Thoreau's transcendental usage pivots on his implicit redefinition of *obscurity*. Things may be "obscure" for two reasons: from a want of accuracy from below or the presence of subtlety from above. Even precise knowledge, when it excludes growth, becomes ignorance, so that in this case *obscurity overhead* makes room for a higher clarity. We should expect as much, because *attain* is a positive word not ordinarily applied to *obscurity*. The juxtaposition of the two follows the same pattern as Thoreau's repenting of his good behavior. Once more, the Janus principle reveals the machinery of transcendental logic, where unlearning certainties outgrows the demands of small-minded credibility.

In these and many other instances, however, Thoreau is not playing the tiresome Chestertonian game of binary paradox. He is not simply saying everything backwards because he cannot think of any other way to catch our attention. He moves back and forth between two graduated levels of reference, far beyond the shock technique of playing the concrete and conventional against the abstract and novel. His dialectic abandons the lower level of immediate perceptions, recognizes a second, and integrates both into a third. As readers, we may first admire the sparks flying from Thoreau's verbal pyrotechnics, turning his wit, irony, and what looks like an addiction to easy contradiction into what he dismisses as little reading. But then, chastened by the grand message of his shooting stars, and by our own lack of "skill in extracting or inserting a moral," we feel, or should feel, "a faint blush on one or both cheeks."

Thoreau does not, of course, rely upon any single technique of getting his message across. His means are many and simultaneous, and like a shower of meteors spread across the sky, they are difficult to see all at once. The stars are there but—as we are told—it is up to us to read them. But the difficulties of his language speak consistently to our higher nature, which he hopes will remember *Walden* at night. Not infrequently, his challenging appeals break into open pronouncement, such as "but men labor under a mistake." Reversing the goals and language of Francis Bacon, Thoreau is not afraid to remind us that "through mere ignorance and mistake" we miss the "finer fruits" as well as the "finest qualities of our nature," which "can be preserved only by the most delicate handling." Thoreau equates ignorance and rigidity; and he comes very close to listing the mob of specific hardnesses of heart within that rob us of what he calls our "elasticity." And this vital suppleness includes not only the flexibility of our imagination, but also the actual capacity to resume our former spiritual shape. Ignorance and rigidity commit a double larceny that reduces the average person to "but the slave and prisoner of his opinion of himself."

Thoreau does not rest in such moral barrage, open or covert. One of his shells in this spiritual civil war is loaded, as we know, with the formula for escape from these "keen and subtle masters that enslave both North and South." When we return to this philosophical charge, we can see that Thoreau has more in mind than *post*-Adamic humanity, when he asks of the laboring man who "has no time to be anything but a machine": "How can he remember well his ignorance—which his growth requires—who has so often to use his knowledge?"

Even in this pivotal question, which presents the formula for mental growth, Thoreau maintains his verbal virtuosity. To *remember his ignorance* sounds backward and smaller. And what is knowledge for if not to *use*? The art of this sentence dazzles, in its own right, in its application to *Walden*, and in its relevance to centuries of history. But the diamond of truth must be recovered from the semiprecious stuff of irony. It is a false step to admire and to go no further. *Walden* is first-rate speleology of the Platonic kind, but with a Yankee twist: we should begin to remember our ignorance now, "in the unfathomed mammoth cave of this world." When we plunge headfirst into Thoreau's style and "come to a hard bottom and rocks in place," *Walden* may feel like a dark and somber tome. After all, Thoreau's book is an instrument for unearthing truth, and in the beginning we should expect to get our hands dirty and to work in the dark.

This juncture requires precision. We have to ask ourselves what *new* and *old* really mean. *Walden* does not—indeed, could not—say anything new in the ordinary sense of the word, where *new* means little more than different and novel. We can see from this that anyone who complains that Thoreau at heart is just another gloomy, anxiety-ridden Puritan has missed the point widely. Thoreau is not derivative because there is only one eternally new thing to say, and he lets us know it: "not all books ... are as dull as their readers." *Walden*'s great originality lies in its escape from the little originality of the Renaissance *personality*. Thoreau writes on that level of communication where the message becomes the messenger and there is no property among ideas— where the "spectator ... is no more I than it is you."

In the human condition which produced the Middle Ages, to be a person was more difficult than it is now, as the psychological pioneer Chaucer confirms so clearly in his poetry. The collective forces of society were still stronger than the individual. But a lot of psychological history has transpired since Chaucer's time; and the situation has been reversed, so that the difficulty has been—until very recently, perhaps—to avoid being a person. From Thoreau's transcendental point of view, nonetheless, all idiosyncratic and therefore partial truths of a merely personal kind are nothing but self-indulgence and delusion, generated by erected wit and fallen will, happily or unhappily as the case may be. His understanding of the individual is galaxies away from what is now called a person.

Here we can also see that Thoreau's style is much more than a pastiche of undigested Eastern mysticism. Reading a number of Near and Far Eastern books did not turn him into an imitation Hindu or Sufi. Quite the contrary, Thoreau is no more "Eastern" than Hindus or Muslims are "Thoreauvian," as he is careful to point out: "Our buckets as it were grate together in the same well. The pure Walden water is mingled with the sacred water of the Ganges." All truth has a common, timeless source. Moreover, the view advanced by Thoreau, that the world is a magical but real "illusion," what the Hindus call *māyā*, has not always been unknown or unimportant in the West. Up until the Renaissance, and even later among gnostic movements, similar ideas were still very much part of the tradition. Western thought, it is safe to say, encompasses many lines of development, and naive materialism has not always been the dominant philosophy.

On the other hand, although perennial ideas shape Thoreau's style, he is much less of a mere Platonist than Emerson, in the narrow sense in which this word is commonly used. He is the last thing from an abstract idealist, because his words mark palpable and generative experiences as well as ideas. For Thoreau—actually more than many a scientific linguist—accepts language for the solid thing that on one level it necessarily must be. At the same time, however, he acknowledges and works on several other levels on which words become spiritual bodies. He himself complains that "in this part of the world it is considered a ground for complaint if a man's writings admit of more than one interpretation." There is in his writing a transcendental, as well as material, empiricism, a supernatural as well as a natural naturalism. An understanding of the working of words, therefore, which cross these boundaries, requires more than the Lockean view of knowledge as sense perception and association. Thoreau's language implies ranking rather than random.

Although Thoreau acknowledges the fall of language into the limitations of flesh and blood, he never presumes that in this tumble words became arbitrary signs. He is not a semioticist and, as he tells us, does "not suppose a case, but takes the case that is," namely, that language is much more than associative algebra. "Things do not change," he reminds us, "we change." Language follows life, so that the very nature of our words, as expressions of ourselves and our connections to this world, also changes. Obviously, Thoreau acknowledges the ordinary mechanisms of language and makes very good use of them. But if language is a machine, it is a very marvelous one indeed, one which has no moving parts. Because it is not made of things, as most people think of things, but comprises an articulated condition which, for all its subtleties, remains before us as an object to be used. To speak more narrowly, language is another *machina mundi*, each part of which is a unique condition. Movement among these parts consists of refinement of being and thus transformation of meaning.

Such facts of transcendental literacy as these often perplex readers who would account for Thoreau's style on the Lockean level. But metaphysical compatibility is the key to his diction and imagery. In the long run, the dilemma of recurring misinterpretation, which seems invariably to attach itself to any attempt to communicate something radically new, supplies its own answer. The "hard bottom and rocks in place," on which we stub our intellectual toes, work to make us feel and eventually see the many connections among Thoreau's mind, his language, and the nature of his argument. His relentless efforts to precipitate this communicative predicament, in order to overcome it, accounts for his primary technique of repetition and variation. In *Walden* Thoreau speaks of his symbolic pond as Donne in his *Satires* speaks of truth. Donne says he "about must and about must go," while Thoreau says he would "go round and round it as long as I live." Through exhaustive figurative restatement he makes his points with a mathematical precision.

A straightforward description of his argument is out of the question, because his is really no argument at all. We do not run into long series of inferences and syllogisms, but rather we find the embodiment of successive conditions. Martin Heidegger says "science does not think." Neither does ordinary logic, when thinking involves grasping new ideas rather than manipulating large numbers of old ones. The logic of science merely applies existing modes of thought; a new theory is an imaginative breakthrough into a new frame of reference. Logic must always assume a single modality of fact and reason within it. *Walden* never does this, for "In sane moments we regard only the facts, the case that is." Thoreau, therefore, proceeds by way of experience—batteries of examples, striking images, metaphors, inversions, ironies, puns, and many a paraphrase. His meaning does not run parallel to his words but rises at right angles to them. *Internal* resonance among homological ideas and images, more than syllogism or statistics, accounts for the cumulative impact of his pages. Thoreau tells it like it is, in as many ways as he can, and then simply says it!

Very early he warns us that "there are more secrets in my trade than in most men's." We should not expect too "many communicable or scholar-like thoughts," because he is trying to say "at present unutterable things." This effort leads to the grand autobiographical parable of the "artist in the city of Kouroo." Drawing upon the Indian epic *Mahā-bhārata*, Thoreau re-imagines the ancestor of the Kauruvas as a man who, in striving to make something as simple as a perfect walking stick, discovered he "had made a new system," "a world with full and fair proportions," because his "material" and "art" were "pure," so that the "result" was "wonderful"—like *Walden*. Even after asking "But why do I stay to mention these things?" Thoreau does stop again to say something more about the problem of communication itself, in order to say everything again. "I fear chiefly," he says, "lest my expression may not be *extra-vagant* enough, may not wander far enough beyond the narrow limits of my daily experience, so as to be adequate to the truth of which I have been convinced." To put it in a more popular way, the functional structure of *Walden* resonates with a transcendental anticipation of the legendary line from *Casablanca*: "Play it [again], Sam."

Thoreau is vigilant never merely to chop logic and thus topple his own kind of argument. He argues by moving among the logics generated by the negative, positive, and integrative dynamics of his mind. Insofar as any one logic is a mood materialized into a thinking-machine, this really amounts to moving from world to world, until like Thoreau's "graceful hawk," we rise through "fields of air" to real heaven. Thoreau likes the word *ethereal*, but the more than dialectical energy of his style may also be described less metaphorically as a *metalogic of progressive refinement*. On the macro-level of full chapters, "Reading," to repeat, is not contradicted by "Sounds," for sound itself can be read as "the language which all things and events speak without metaphor." The result of this larger harmony is the ability to read a higher language. Nor is "Sounds" canceled by the silence of "Solitude," for solitude allows us "to begin to find" and thus to read ourselves; nor is "Solitude" violated by the arrival of spiritual "Visitors," for then we communicate with other "honest pilgrims" from "unexplored and uncultivated continents on the other side" "of the great ocean of solitude." Thoreau's logics change from chapter to chapter.

Likewise on the micro-level of single words and phrases, *repent* does not contradict, but redefines *good behavior*, for it implies the abandonment of good for better behavior. In the same vein, Thoreau jokes that he has not *attained to obscurity*, because higher truths are obscure and any truth not obscure to his unimaginative neighbors is not likely to be very high. The progress of Thoreau's book never subsumes, but rather includes and transforms. Each part surmounts "the enterprises of another like stranded vessels," but always builds nobler communicative structures in Nautilus fashion.

The artist in the city of Kouroo carves a nobler walking stick and, in so doing, achieves a timeless universe: "As he made no compromise with Time, Time kept out of his way," indeed, time kindly stopped for Thoreau because he could not stop for time. In terms of communication, such timelessness, or at least such other modes of time than linear sequence in space, works sea changes on language. Words wash up on the furthest shores of the mind, where they are de*posited* in experience of the *finest sediment* of meaning. In Thoreau's world honest mental pilgrims are, of course, walkers; and since Thoreau has already told us "My head is hands and feet," we should not be surprised to find him allegorizing the journeys of the mind:

In our most trivial walks, we are constantly, though unconsciously, steering like pilots by certain well-known beacons and headlands, and if we go beyond our usual course we still carry in our minds the bearing of some neighboring cape; and not till we are completely lost, or turned round,—for a man needs only to be turned round once with his eyes shut in this world to be lost,—do we appreciate the vastness and strangeness of nature.

This frequent use of the familiar *headlands* of knowledge does not allow the "laboring man" to "remember well his ignorance." Our usual course tells us again that "the surface of the earth is soft and impressible by the feet of men; and so with the paths which the mind travels."

In such a style, which makes frequent use of homological identities, repetition becomes homogeneity, argument turns into example, and development into growth. As we will see, synonymity and equivalence become major architectonic forces in Thoreau's book. His warning that there is more than one way to skin a cat is representative:

This is the only way, we say; but there are as many ways as there can be drawn radii from one centre. All change is a miracle to contemplate; but it is a miracle which is taking place every instant. Confucius said, "To know that we know what we know, and that we do not know what we do not know, that is true knowledge." When one man has reduced a fact of the imagination to be a fact to his understanding, I foresee that all men will at length establish their lives on that basis.

Here the *metalogic of progressive refinement* demands that we use our heads for "an organ of burrowing," "begin to mine" more deeply, and go even lower and deeper.

Two graduated levels of consciousness are focused by Thoreau's language. His qualification *we say* is more than a conversational tag and implies what others who are wiser say to the contrary. The *radii from one center* move from moral assertion to concrete example and expand the deeper meaning of *only*. *All change* universalizes the *miracle* of particular experience, and *every instant* renders life immediately and decisively sacred. *Confucius said* then adds the authority of universal tradition to clear thinking in the present. And finally, the movement between *imagination* and *fact* along the necessary axis of the *I* of *one man* confirms the need and source of right action and its inevitable results. The adverbial phrase *at length*, in addition, reminds us that Thoreau is still plastering the house of *Walden* and again inviting us to "lie at [our] length" on his book as a *basis*. The immediate result is a virtuosity of persuasion which *transforms* rather than argues, as precise in its logic*s* as it is profound in its imagination.

In Thoreau's case, therefore, the critical platitude does establish the fact that the style is the man, and the man is the book. Thoreau lived as he thought, wrote as he lived. The result is an inimitably Swiftian cogency: "Proper words in proper places, makes the true Definition of Style." On every path through *Walden* woods we meet a vital mingling of idea, language, and form, in which the *what* and *how* of Thoreau's style walk hand in hand.

5

THE SUBTLE AND
UNSUBTLE GUMPHUS

Walden's first six chapters deserve another look—there is more to say. But *another* look should be understood to mean a *new* rather than only a *longer* look from the same point of view. More of the same will not do. For in *Walden* one chapter is never just tacked on to another, but joined more subtly as in the Middle Ages the soul was believed to be fastened to the body by a special kind of little pin called a *gumphus*.[1] Each part in Thoreau's machine of the world is fastened to the next with connections subtle enough to pin the soul to the flesh. But those who feel that another look and a longer sojourn circling the same territory are unnecessary should "turne over the leef," as Chaucer says, "and chese another tale." Thoreau nods in agreement: "If you are acquainted with the principle, what do you care for a myriad instances and applications?"

Those for whom this *you* fits should proceed to the next chapter, for Thoreau does not "prescribe rules ... to those who are well employed." But some may be less familiar than others with *Walden*, or less confident in the summary so far advanced, so that they may wish to pin down a few

---

1. Latin for "a pin, a little nail," from the Greek *gomphos*, "a large wedge-shaped bolt or nail, for ship building; any bond or fastening"; plural, *gomphoi*, "the cross-ribs of Egyptian canoes," thus allegorically the "chest" or "[rib]cage," which contains the soul and thus catches holy ghosts.

more instances of the "infinite number of profiles, though absolutely but one form" *Walden* displays. They should read on.

Certainly, trying to rank *Walden*'s several major sections does not make much sense, because one group of chapters is not more important than another. Yet the progression from section to section does have a cumulative effect, and any explanation of *Walden* as a report must take this into account. Looking back may also justify a specific order of inquiry, because *Walden* is a report which is more than reportorial. Its paralogical subject and method involve real change and do not lend themselves to obvious, straightforward sequences.

Nonetheless, a good argument can be made that the first six steps in *Walden* are the most important, because well begun is half done. With these behind or rather within them, people can work out the next two groups for themselves. Thoreau's book, moreover, *is* consummately organized. In writing it, he made a large number of detailed changes through seven versions. It does not make any sense to presume that his revisions were not guided by a plan and that the outcome of this plan is neither accessible nor important. It turns out, that "Economy" and the next five chapters are in fact uniquely introductory in a number of interlocking ways, even though they can be taken up only one at a time. Another look, then, at *Walden*'s first six chapters, turns naturally to the *specific* functions of each chapter. If too avid a local interest is allowed to displace their larger purpose and effect, of course, there is a danger that art might displace Thoreau's artistry, which aims at truth and goodness as well as beauty.

Walden presumes the possibility of knowledge rather than the necessity of ignorance. For this reason agnostic romantic approaches are not very useful for understanding how *Walden* actually works. When endless groping through ignorance is mistaken for arriving at truth, art and the personality become indistinguishable, and the actual progress of the book's transcendental argument becomes inaccessible. Approaches that altogether deny the existence of any text are worse than useless. The self that the "gropers" are forever fondling is the handy lower one; they never arrive at anything higher, and end up insisting that even old Adam is unknowable. To be sure, Thoreau also talks in terms of "discovery" and "self," but *his* transcendental discoveries, as he tells us, "were not by the synthetic but analytic process." His transcendental method is properly experimental, but it is not "groping" when this means an endless game of blindman's buff into the valley of convenient ignorance. He knows where he is going, how to get there, and he plans on arriving. He never gets *up* mixed up with *down*, nor does he confuse the light of genuine inspiration with the phosphorescent glow of psychic disintegration.

So far, then, a close look shows that Thoreau has diagnosed his reader's chief ailment as a mortally definite strain of three-dimensional dementia. This wrong-headed fixity of mind leads to *rigor mortis* of being, even before death, and to future complications. We can follow the course of Thoreau's urgent, pre-inquest treatment, as he seeks to cure the patient, who has slipped into a coma of "quiet desperation." Medical analogies are fitting, for as Chaucer also reminds us, there is "phisicien but oon" who can cure the terminal disease that Thoreau and his co-authors have in mind. With the cure compounded, and the first dosage administered, he operates according to plan, warning his patient reader that the treatment is not going to be easy, since "there are more secrets in my trade than in most men's ... as demand a universal knowledge." Thoreau does not gloss over the severity of the malady, and this honesty anticipates his therapy: to rattle his reader's self-imposed cage, so the holy ghost can escape. Recovery is gradual, then seemingly instantaneous, like the coming of spring. Health arrives step-by-step, as "Hebe, cup-bearer to Jupiter," enters with the elixir that opens up the narrowness that binds us to the world of surfaces. We do "stretch the seams" of space as we regain our lost elasticity. As Thoreau prescribes, the metaphysics of this *meta*morphosis entail fine distinctions.

Thoreau's medicine for the mind can now be reformulated more precisely. The first ingredient of his prescription names the scene of the crime, and this is Renaissance *space*. We cage ourselves in an unconscious belief that surfaces determine reality. Eliminating this visual fixation provides the fulcrum of many of *Walden*'s well-known tropes. We "survey the world through a telescope or a microscope, and never with [the] natural eye," so that "Through an infirmity of our natures," he adds, "we suppose a case, and put ourselves into it, and hence are in two cases at the same time, and it is doubly difficult to get out." The common leverage of Thoreau's imagery, whether mercantile, agricultural, sartorial, architectural, or auroral, works to pry us out of this manifold hall of mirrors. Escape from the glistening opacity of ordinary space and time into the ethereal clarity of the eternal present establishes another, possibly central, measure of the kaleidoscopic metamorphoses through which the language and thought of *Walden* pass. There is indeed no "visible inlet or outlet" to Walden Pond, "except by the clouds and evaporation." There is no logical ladder out of life's dilemmas. We must, as it were, distill the stuff of Thoreau's images and follow the rising vapors.

A fully unencumbered sense of space opens into the higher senses of *Walden*. Thoreau psychologizes each kind of place into a condition of being. Each mode of experience is generated by a point of view understood as a form of knowledge. From the very beginning, therefore, Thoreau works relentlessly on where we are "said to live." He speaks of being "confined to this theme by the narrowness of my experience," reports "from a distant land," warns specifically of not "stretch[ing] the seams in putting on the coat," talks about our "outward condition," says he has "travelled a great deal in Concord," speaks of those who inch across "the breadth of vast empires," and other interesting places.

There is hardly a page in *Walden* on which Thoreau does not try to convince us of the "vastness and strangeness of nature" and "the infinite extent of our relations." His central message is hyperspatial: "Olympus is but the outside of earth everywhere." For example, only by once more putting the question *where* in the Chapter "Visitors," can we appreciate the overlay of metaphysics and autobiography in the "woodchopper" and "village idiot." Thoreau's wood-chopping friend Therien signifies the animal in every one of us, including Thoreau. As such he also represents the problem of integrating this animal nature with the intellect and, by extension, the task of educating humanity in general, the "village idiot" of the universe. Therien, thus, also epitomizes the problem of communication. This we can see when Thoreau complains, "Yet I never, by any maneuvering, could get him to take the spiritual view of things." Here we learn a great deal about what kind of a book *Walden* is and what kind of readers Thoreau expects it to have. If we change pronouns in this sentence, and read *us* for *him*, we begin to see what kind of communicative maneuvering informs the stylistic virtuosity of *Walden*. The *locus* of the confrontation reveals the *significatio*. After we have realized how far Thoreau has led us into his own space, we can grasp the full power and leverage of "MEANWHILE my beans," which introduces his second group of chapters. Both the shape and the workings of *Walden* are aimed at creating an "elastic and vigorous thought." "To read well ... is a noble exercise," precisely because the "tumbling" and "ethereal flight" of transcendental gymnastics requires great suppleness of mind. Anyone who is a "prisoner of his own opinion of himself" is unlikely to make record-breaking metaphysical leaps. In *Walden* we learn by doing—the right things.

Each step in the refinement of space becomes the means to another, leading ultimately to a full identification of *space* and *mind*. At first, in "Economy," references to space are indirect and contrived so as to be no more than acceptably metaphorical. *Walden* opens with a locative specificity tantamount to a plotting of coordinates. At first, there is little in the opening epitome to make us suspect unusual connotations, as in the verb *obtrude*, for example, which he uses to describe the presentation of his experiences. But it is in the nature of things that we enter the enchanted wood unawares and find ourselves *thrust* into another space. And as Thoreau's elusive spiritual duplicity begins to work, the shifting landscape causes us to check the lenses in our own bifocals, in order to see the sly humor residing in the tardily recognized import of his spatial language. Later, we also discover that the word *bulk* does not refer so much to the greater part as it does to the material part, Thoreau's *residual statement.*

Walden's first paragraph comprises a paradigm of the entire work, as the most literal description of what Thoreau did: "WHEN I wrote the following pages, or rather the bulk of them, I lived alone, in the woods, a mile from any neighbor, in a house which I had built myself, on the shore of Walden Pond, in Concord, Massachusetts, and earned my living by the labor of my hands only." Here Thoreau's honesty is also his sarcasm. He does in fact tell the whole truth, but we soon learn that "alone, in the woods, a mile from any neighbor, in a house" in no way describes the location of the real *Walden* adventure.[2] For very soon he introduces a distinction between "how I have desired to spend my life" and "its actual history." Comprehending the polarity of spiritual as well as material truth—and the unity of the two—affords no small portion of the pleasure and a great deal of the reason for reading *Walden*. We can see from a new perspective that such spatial phrases as being "confined to this theme by the narrowness of my experience," not "stretch[ing] the seams in putting on this coat," reporting to our kindred "from a distant land," and having "travelled a good deal in Concord," all and in more than one sense point to where Thoreau, as we might say, is coming from. Quite apart from his higher literalism, a full appreciation of Thoreau's literary virtuosity depends upon an imaginative and elastic sense of space.

The joke is kept for a number of pages and through a significant battery of telling but double-edged images. References to "outward" riches and "inward" poverty, to time "spent outside the town," and to his "place," and so on, lead to a single yardstick for "distance, whether of space or time," and even further to a conflation of space, morality, and metaphysics in the painful truth that "the bad neighborhood to be avoided is our own scurvy selves." Indeed, in a very ancient way, Thoreau gradually homologizes cosmos, house, and human body, when he urges us to consider "what foundation a door, a window, a cellar, a garret, have in the nature of man." And in so doing he provides, in addition to broad hints at the way these architectural categories will be allegorized, still another spatial resolution of human faculties. He talks of tents, for example, as the best of artificial dwellings. But even his own tent proved insufficiently ethereal and *re*movable, so that it too had to be abandoned, "still rolled up in my garret," as he

---

2. Two neighbors, actually, lived within less than a mile.

proceeded on his way, like the smoke from his chimney, to higher regions. In *Walden* a "handkerchief" will do "for a shed."

Thoreau closes "Economy" with a general appeal to live a free life like "the azads, or religious independents," who neither flourish nor fade, and this image again links new spaces with new lives. An implicit equivalence between mental condition and quality of space is resumed with even greater energy in "Where I Lived, and What I Lived For." Here he repeats his warning, "As long as possible live free and uncommitted," but does so in a context which psychologizes space, so that point for point correlates with the hidden potential of physical restrictions. Thoreau undertakes the difficult task of explaining how we can *locate* somewhere and not be caught and caged there. He accomplishes this feat by way of the mind as a remedy for the confinements of place. He slips through the net of ownership by means of imaginary purchases. "In imagination," Thoreau tells us, "I have bought all the farms.... The present was my next experiment of this kind." The phrase "this kind" leaves little doubt, at least in Thoreau's archetypal geography, where a house fit for a "travelling god" will be located. It will not be found in the "bad neighborhood" which is "our own scurvy selves," but on "Olympus," which, as he has told us, is everywhere. Clearly, Thoreau's choice of words with unusual connotations, his recapitulation of cosmogony, and his recollection of existential mysteries are phenomenologically central to both the method and message of his spatial idiom.

The second "... and What I Lived For" half of this second and symbolically locative chapter completes the existential conflation of ordinary time and space. Thoreau confirms that "both time and place were changed, and I dwelt nearer to those parts of the universe and to those eras of history which most attracted me." He quickly adds, however, that this conditional location is neither static nor passive. Its swiftly undulating permanence stands like a waterfall's stony arch or like flames, which also co-exist with a rushing movement of the matter they contain. To reach and remain in such a place, mentally, we must keep forever on the move. Location and condition, place and mind, coincide only through an unwavering and vital wakefulness, since "to him whose elastic and vigorous thought keeps pace with the sun, the day is a perpetual morning.... To be awake is to be alive." Thoreau marries his description to our experience and thereby spans the gulf between merely thinking about it and actually living it. Precisely this split defines, again, what *Walden* would have us overcome, so that we may co-author life as well as read about it.

People who persist in separating thinking from living abuse his art for the purpose of making their "low condition comfortable." Popping down a handful of "God's Drops," they strive to understand without applying and, to some extent, to enjoy without accepting his book. But Thoreau's sole purpose is to oblige everyone "to solve the problems of life, not only theoretically, but practically." He did not write *Walden* to be read in the way Christianity has sometimes been adopted, "merely as an improved method of *agri*-culture." He would never *agree* to recalling God by common consent. *Walden* is not little reading like our insurance policies. Remembering that space is a condition forms the ontological basis for resacralizing this profaned world and its inhabitants.

"Reading," "Sounds," and "Solitude," as it has been suggested, follow in a step-by-step refinement of our consciousness. The instrument of this transformation is a progressive etherealization and reanimation of "Where I Lived." The mishmash of ordinary perception evaporates and spirals into higher facts. First the dregs of little reading are siphoned off, and its publishers and their reader-accomplices are condemned. "If others are the machines to provide this provender, they are the machines to read it." Next, great books are distilled into their normal best. "For what are classics," he asks, "but the noblest recorded thoughts of man?" But just when we feel that for once we are on the same side of a question as Thoreau, shapeshifter as he is, like his own loon he surfaces in another place, takes everything back, disagrees, presents greater proof, and condemns *all* reading from a stronger and far more rarified position. The best books, he goes on to say in "Sounds," are acceptable as far as they go, but they do not go far enough.

> But while we are confined to books, though the most select and classic, and read only particular written languages, which are themselves but dialects and provincial, we are in danger of forgetting the language which all things and events speak without metaphor, which alone is copious and standard. Much is published, but little printed.

Pursuing his spatial idiom with the words *confined* and *provincial*, Thoreau brings together much of what he has already said in other ways about communication. Reading words can reach only as far as can the reader, across the boundary between direct and indirect knowledge.

In "Solitude" the transfer of knowledge that communication implies is resolved through an elimination of space and, therefore, of both the direct and indirect means it sustains. By closing the gap between the knower and the known, Thoreau eliminates the process of knowing. An openly mystical union renders the process impossible and the question irrelevant, and we wake, as he says later, "to an answered question, to Nature and daylight." Beyond time and space there can be no distance "whether of space or time" and, therefore, no room nor need for any means. The

Voice of the Silence talks to itself and bears the same relation to language as language does to mere sounds. Thoreau
rises along a spiraling course to reading the *Logos* itself.

> This carload of torn sails is more legible and interest-
> ing now than if they should be wrought into paper and
> printed books. Who can write so graphically the history
> of storms they have weathered as these rents have
> done? .... And hark! here comes the cattle-train bear-
> ing the cattle of a thousand hills ... drovers with their
> sticks, and shepherd boys in the midst of their flocks.

And from reading the great world-symbol in its grand complexity and thundering eloquence—before its lofty history
is written *down* on mere paper—Thoreau proceeds, via the
Psalms, into a mystical reading of the unmanifest portion of
himself, which he describes as "the presence and criticism
of a part of me, which, as it were, is not a part of me, but
spectator, sharing no experience, but taking note of it, and
that is no more I than it is you." These two important passages, from "Sounds" and "Solitude," are replete with sug-
gestions for understanding the subtlety of Thoreau's
concern with communication.

They show that he has turned his ear away from the
"confused *tintinnabulum* from without ... the noise of my
contemporaries," to listen to the silence itself. This epistemological gesture moves from the peak of conceptual experience, represented by the classics, to a participation in
the "vibration of the universal lyre" and a union with the
"one articulation of Nature," as both merge into a union
that subsumes the working of his own book. The first-per-
son narrator and the second-person reader and the message between them are left without a spatial basis at the
apex of the spiritual triangle. Thoreau's threefold
method, with its denials, refinements, and acceptances,

has succeeded in saying "at present unutterable things" and concludes in a conscious grasp of truths formerly thought to be so mystical as to be "unutterable." Method itself is transcended, interestingly enough, before in the hands of diligent German mediocrity, as Paul Valéry warned, it conquered the rest of the nineteenth century and much of the twentieth.

But this New England *samādhi* cannot be prolonged, even by an enlightened Thoreau, not without serious difficulties, because his all too actual readers, like "humbler esculents," have not had many occasions to mature and are, therefore, not in the habit of flowering. They tend rather to forget their heads and remember their roots, and the need of tangible earth. Not quite up to following Thoreau's advice to "invert your head," they cannot remain too long upside down even when they try to follow Thoreau's advice and burrow headfirst into books like *Walden.* The prospect of seeing "a double shadow of [themselves], one standing on the head of the other" is too frightening. This peak experience is needed, nonetheless, as a useful preview of higher goals and also as a guide to reading the rest of *Walden.* Otherwise, without this moment of insight, the effort of *Walden*'s first six chapters would be wasted, and practical communication would fall apart for want of a *tertium quid.* Pegasus grounded for want of one subtle *gumphus.*

If we could maintain such an altitude, we would read no further but begin to co-author *Walden* and, perhaps, to rewrite the more Platonic Emerson. The continuation of *Walden* argues Thoreau's thoughts on the matter. These insights from his meditative summit conference must be turned back upon the world, where we actually live and read. Thoreau is neither a linguistic nor theological Monophysite. He turns his sights upon us with a multidimensional question, "What sort of space is that which separates a man from his fellows and makes him solitary?" "Any prospect of awakening or coming to life to a dead man makes indifferent all times and places." Thoreau urges every modern Lazarus to forget about burying himself and to remember "the precept of the old philosopher ... Explore thyself." Here and now is the place to begin. "Let us settle ourselves ... till we come to a hard bottom and rocks in place, which we can call *reality*, and say, This is, and no mistake; and then begin." Such spatial language squares the circle of learning. Space—*kha* in Sanskrit—is also mind.

Space engages the common denominator of bodily experience, so that the tape of life and the music of the spheres it has recorded can be played back. If our space can be restored "to the vigor of youth" and made to dance again, so then the mental *cases* we *put ourselves into* can be reopened, so that we can trace a new map of the world. "This is the only way, we say; but there are as many ways as there can be drawn radii from one centre." This magical idea, as we have seen, most explicit and active in *Walden*'s early chapters, continues to operate throughout the book.

> In our most trivial walks, we are constantly, though unconsciously, steering like pilots by certain well-known beacons and headlands, and if we go beyond our usual course we still carry in our minds the bearings of some neighboring cape; and not until we are completely lost, or turned round,—for a man needs only to be turned round once with his eyes shut in this world to be lost,—do we appreciate the vastness and strangeness of nature. Every man has to learn the points of the compass again as often as he awakes, whether from sleep or any abstraction. Not till we are lost, in other words not till we have lost the world, do we begin to find ourselves, and realize where we are and the infinite extent of our relations.

This passage, from "The Village," confirms Thoreau's relentless insistence upon the identity of mind, space, and experience.

The message is timeless, and Thoreau's pun on the *headlands*, geographic and mental, tells us that the world is indeed, as Schopenhauer remembered, made of will and ideas as well as rocks. Since unwavering awareness and active memory are essential for "effective intellectual exertion," Thoreau never allows the language of *Walden* to lapse into convention. "With thinking," he adds in "Solitude," "we may be beside ourselves in a sane sense."

> I had withdrawn so far within the great ocean of solitude, into which the rivers of society empty, that for the most part, so far as my needs were concerned, only the finest sediment was deposited around me. Beside, there were wafted to me evidences of unexplored and uncultivated continents on the other side.

Just at this convenient moment, of course, "visitors" arrive as representatives, we imagine, of the *finest sediment*, to sit in Thoreau's house. And once more the *where* of everything changes everything, including Thoreau's several thematic metaphors and the new channels opened by this fluviatile imagery.

As *Walden* flows toward the *great ocean of solitude*, Thoreau's spatial idiom takes on the character of a pervasive given which we can put to new communicative uses, more as an insight that we have made our own, than as a lesson still to be learned. Thoreau's language of space grows less insistent, but is never unimportant nor silent. This we can see in the first chapter of *Walden*'s second section, "The Bean-Field," where cultivation links the business at hand to the locus of language itself. Language grows out of the earth, "as some must work in fields if only for the sake of

tropes and expression, to serve a parable-maker one day."
And since in Thoreau's day much of Africa was unexplored, left blank, and colored white on the map, in "Conclusion" he can return to a direct and vigorous spatial
idiom and ask, "What does Africa,—what does the West
stand for? Is not our own interior white on the chart?" The
directness of this not-to-be-put-off question confirms the
overall movement of *Walden* from right imagination to fact.
Whatever Thoreau first expresses figuratively he later states
outright, according to a graduated dialectic. Opposition to
the "most sacred laws of society" is justified only through
"obedience to yet more sacred laws."

In the second and third sections of *Walden,* and especially
in the very last chapter "Conclusion," Thoreau turns his interest in communication upon his own book in a way that
multiplies its sophistication. His telling remark that most
people are "convicted by the wisdom of one good book, the
Bible," suggests that he is writing another such *good book.*
His gnomic allusions, further, to Revelation 1:16 in "Reading," such as, "*There* are the stars, and they who can may
read them," enter into a highly symbolic and abstruse play
upon "Walden," pond and book, and crystalize into an explicit but often misunderstood statement that he has written in cipher. "It is a ridiculous demand which England
and America make, that you shall speak so that they can understand you.... I desire to speak somewhere *without*
bounds ... but in this part of the world it is considered a
ground for complaint if a man's writings admit of more
than one interpretation." The pun in the phrase "*without*
bounds" says it all spatially. Thoreau would speak with un-
trammeled openness, so that he will not be obliged to make
embarrassing leaps of illogic. His *more than one* means
higher and more subtle, not merely alternative senses as
aesthetic minds who still prefer "Cambridge ice" would
have it. Thoreau's "Conclusion" is, indeed, Emersonian in

its declarative force; but it also shows, most clearly of all perhaps, his keen and paradoxical struggle to utter "unutterable things." There, point for point and in so many words, he follows his own advice, placing "foundations" under his "castles in the air," as he rewords the metaphors of "Economy" into literal conclusions. The intensity of his own vision made him impatient always to be speaking "communicable or scholar-like thoughts," "so that they understand you," and we can understand why on occasion he did "despair of getting anything quite simple and honest done in this world by the help of men."

Yet the disciplined desire to drive his point home tempered and directed Thoreau's frustration. He never forgets the difference between an ordinary nail and a *gumphus*, and this enabled him to hammer out a book for "our condition exactly." Accordingly, he accepts the narrow boundaries of ordinary three-dimensional space as his starting point. From this condition, to which ordinary men have pinned their hopes with many an unsubtle *gumphus*, he proceeds to pry us free by opening our bounds into boundless mind. The result is *Walden*, which, like Christ to Christians, becomes "a lower heaven itself so much the more important" to readers whom he wishes to transform into co-authors.

6
COLERIDGE'S
"LOST LETTER"

English romanticism should never be confused with American transcendentalism. The two are quite different. Both movements were intensely felt, to be sure, and both were reactions against the materialism of the eighteenth century. But romanticism, for all its mystical moments and Wordsworthian "spots of time," in subtle ways actually extends the eighteenth century. At bottom it clings to an empirical view of nature more as a mirror to reflect human emotions and less as a partner "to carve and paint the very atmosphere and medium through which we look." Transcendentalism, on the other hand, less entangled in the ropes and pulleys of the Lockean view of knowledge, commands a greater than psychological seriousness and displays a genuine, if sometimes obscure, religious energy. Yet in a broad historical sense, men like the English romantic Samuel Taylor Coleridge and the American transcendentalist Thoreau, each in his own way, do react against the material view of mind and being, so that legitimate comparisons can be made.

Their reactions and goals are essentially the same. Coleridge, like Thoreau, rejects the Lockean tradition and tries to communicate metaphysics to materialists. There is, however, one major difference in energy if not in substance. Coleridge gives up, while Thoreau does not. To be sure,

Coleridge must be credited with leading the first charge; but he could not overcome the resistance of British common sense, and retreated. This English retreat and the failure of romanticism to come of age, can tell us a great deal about the American assault and the larger war in which people like Coleridge and Thoreau were engaged. In particular, Coleridge's retreat sheds light on the intellectual weaponry with which Thoreau launches and executes his campaign in the first six chapters of *Walden*. We can see how, at the critical moment, Coleridge abandons his argument as Thoreau never does.

Although we have twice explored the "lower heaven" of *Walden*'s first six chapters, only a few of its significant features have been charted. Huge areas remain blank and white. But a map is only a map; and the very best is never more than a copy of a copy. As powerful as words may be, Owen Barfield reminds us that "meaning itself can never be *conveyed* from one person to another; words are not bottles; every individual must intuit meaning for himself, and the function of the poetic is to mediate such intuition by suitable suggestion." Thoreau can mediate, but we all must be the authors of our own meaning.

At the same time, however, reading *Walden* may be compared to travelling to a distant land, in order to map out the terrain. An abundance of sunrise moments dazzles the sojourner with choices of what to see, what to remember, and what to record and to carry back. And goodness requires that the beauties and truths discovered be shared. Only such hyperbole can begin to encompass what we would hope is not an uncommon *Walden* experience, for as Thoreau says outright, "These same questions ... each has answered them, according to his ability, by his words and his life." As aspiring co-authors of *Walden*, all of us, according to our ability, will see and return with what trophies we can, as poets reading a poet or as star-readers with a stumbling fluency in the universal language C. S. Lewis calls "Old Solar."

Writing about *Walden* becomes "a rare amusement, which, continued too long, might … become a dissipation." Explaining *Walden* emboldens the writer to lay siege to Thoreau's "castles in the air," in order to enjoy the sweet fruition of one's own earthly book. As time passes, however, less and less frequently do the "gross necessaries of life" require us to excuse our omissions by repeating Jonathan Swift's *hic multa desiderantur*. We can now supply many of the desired reasons, because the need to suppress explanations, as Coleridge did, has passed. These days, we no longer need to write abortive romances, like Hawthorne, or pen unscientific postscripts, like Kierkegaard, or unintelligible epics like Blake, or otherwise indulge a strategic vagueness before the scientists of the age. Admittedly, Thoreau did write *Walden* to explain *A Week*, but he was not a man "to practise resignation, unless it was quite necessary." As times change, the hideous strength of cold empiricism flags, and the perennial philosophy is again finding its voice.

Another, Coleridgean look at the now familiar battleground of *Walden*'s first six chapters may seem unduly circular. But as often is the case, the long way around is really the shortest way to the water. Brevity may be measured in many ways besides small numbers of pages, and straight lines are not always the shortest distances between two points worth making. As Thoreau tells us, if we want to relish the "true flavor" of wild berries, "There is only one way to obtain it, yet few take that way," which is the spiral path leading to the pond from "a considerable height." When the subject is transcendental, taking the long way around and sticking to the subject are not easy, but doing so commands a second advantage of escaping the dark tarn of academic criticism.

Otherwise, there is no way to be sure that, as far as this is possible, one has been understood. There is no way around it, with *Walden* it's either sticking to the subject or writing footnotes. The risk, of course, in any attempt to play Prometheus and "to speak somewhere *without* bounds," and to say "what you have to say, not what you ought," is the difficulty, to put it bluntly, of deciding on when to write sideways. What height of experience is neither too high nor too low? What moment is too soon or too late? And for that matter where, in what mansion, will the reader be found? These are the *critical* questions. If there is a miscalculation, a knocking on the wrong door, or a peddling of unpopular baskets to the wrong market or at the wrong season, the best words will be silenced into pantomime. And like Thoreau, his co-authors may end up talking to themselves in a room lined with their own books and listening to the "demoniac laughter" of their own music.

Timing is crucial in all such matters, and Thoreau anticipates us with the question, "How now, Hermit, is it too soon?" And it may be too soon, for it may well be that not enough has happened to human beings since Thoreau scaled Olympus. The aged C. G. Jung was of this opinion, convinced that "we have reached the limit of our evolution—the point from which we can advance no further. Man started from an unconscious state and has ever striven for greater and greater consciousness ... and the path along which we are going is merely an extension of it." Technologically speaking, computers are nothing more than highly refined steam engines.

For better or worse, humanity may not have grown and changed enough, to allow for higher perspectives on the unsayable. Often, in this delicate matter of timing, this does seem to be the case. People seem to be rock-bound on the very same ledge where they were all clustered a century or more ago. The *we* of Thoreau's "things do not change;

we change" does not seem to have changed very much in relation to the things of the world, so that more of what the Word is saying cannot be heard. Indeed, permanent, perhaps terminal, materialism still seems to be the rule of the day, especially when we search for new expressions and see how often they lead right back to *Walden* and Thoreau's bean-field.

Nonetheless, as gloomy as the outlook for intelligence may be, a few people have had word-making experiences since *Walden* was composed. Everything does not seem to have happened long ago *in illo tempore*. A new age is always coming of age. Yet on this question too, Thoreau more often than not bests his critics, for the knack is to say the just-right, solid-enough things. He always keeps a sharp eye on the specific gravity of his facts and the density of his reader.

Even though we must follow Thoreau outside the fifth *Veda* of literature and deal directly with the pre-metaphorical realities on which all writing rests, our goal should always be *Walden*, not the history of philosophy or language. Naked truth, passing down through the mind into the peculiar flesh of words, gets spun into the solid stuff of art. But like all bodies, which are necessarily composite, anything which is woven, including written *texts*, may be unravelled. The very existence of a book like *Walden* should put us on our guard. Like any bible, such a book is an embarrassment, because scripture stands as a reminder that the truth is written *down* just before it is forgotten. Such an epochal book as *Walden*, moreover, which digs into the beginning of things and discards tradition in order to start over again—such a book implies little less than the Gordian knot of human history. To quote Thoreau quoting Milton, it engages little less than "fate, free will, [and] foreknowledge absolute." A good book can hardly do otherwise, since "all these times and places and occasions are now and here. God himself culminates in the present moment."

So we are obliged to conclude that, unless Thoreau were an outright fool or just plain mad (and his reputation seems to eliminate these evasions), there must have been some set of circumstances, a nexus of forces against which he waged his transcendental war, some configuration of actual physical, psychical, and spiritual errors he wanted to correct. Understanding *Walden*, therefore, as opposed to superimposing alien ideas upon it, requires an understanding of just what these things were. And such an understanding, in turn, requires nothing less than a lucid, serious, and original relation to "these same questions." What was he really after? What did he try to do?

If contemporary alpinists of the mind are indeed still napping on the same ledge on the cosmic mountain, there can be no new prospects, because the view of the valley world and its fair field full of folk will not enlarge except from a higher view point. Happily, a new age is coming of age, so that this is not the case for everyone. A few more have explored the peak, and returned, and even larger numbers are ascending the trails of these pioneers, so that through the knowledge gained by their combined expeditions we can now speak less metaphorically. We are less obliged to continue to "live meanly, like ants; though the fable tells us that we were long ago changed into men." Through Thoreau's labors with beans and his "work in fields ... for the sake of tropes and expression," many of his imaginations have, at least for awhile, become facts.

Since Thoreau's time, through the like efforts of fellow soldiers—like Coleridge, Søren Kierkegaard, Helena Blavatsky, Paul Valéry, Oswald Spengler, Carl Jung, Mircea Eliade, C. S. Lewis, and Owen Barfield—more may be uttered. It is literally true that the "symbol of an ancient man's thought becomes a modern man's speech." Thoreau's stature is confirmed by the frequency with which his ideas, even his phrases, come to mind when we read these and other like-minded writers among his successors. What else, for representative examples, are Jung's statement, "The world is ever as it has been, but our consciousness undergoes peculiar changes," and Owen Barfield's, "the thing has remained the same, but ... people have come to think differently about it," but less succinct restatements of Thoreau's pungent, "Things do not change; we change"? Such parallels and anticipations are easily multiplied. Echoes of Thoreau, for example, can be heard in C. S. Lewis' use of food imagery. Lewis and Thoreau are remarkably close in their analysis of experience, even to the inspiration one may gain from eating. Thoreau marvels that, "I have been thrilled to think that I owed a mental perception to the commonly gross sense of taste, that I have been inspired through the palate, that some berries which I had eaten on a hillside had fed my genius." Lewis often makes the same use of food, to make a point. Reading better books, for example, produces not more but better pleasure "as if a food one had enjoyed for the taste proved one day to enable you (like dragon's blood) to understand the speech of birds.... Now I know there is something far better—the something that came to me in the smell of the carrot." These and many more examples show clearly that, as far as Thoreau goes, later writers "may be sure that they have been anticipated."

To square this final circling of *Walden*'s first six chapters in a way that will turn polemic imaginings into literary facts, it is helpful to arm ourselves with the experiences, anchored in language, of such people as these, who also have dealt with "these same questions," as we turn directly to the communicative problem Thoreau sought to solve. A step in this direction has already been taken through skirting many a "scholar-like" thought. But at this stage a more inclusive view of history may correct contemporary "psychology," because Thoreau's dialectic parallels the evolution of

Western consciousness. It is always *as above, so below,* and in many ways now as then. Ontogeny does in fact recapitulate phylogeny. "There is a period in the history of the individual, as of the race, when hunters are the 'best'." "Every child begins the world again." The materialistic error is a personal problem long before and after it becomes a cultural crisis.

The telltale strenuousness of Thoreau's efforts to "throw," in his words, "one arch at least over the darker gulf of ignorance which surrounds us" provides a telling example of the connection among individual being, linguistic continuity, and cultural homogeneity, especially in the case of a mind of Thoreau's stature, where particulars take on general significance. If anything to the point is to be said about an individual's attempt to communicate, the connection between society and language must be absolutely clear. We must follow Confucius and first rectify the language.

Specifically, what must be made clear is the give and take between consciousness and meaning. Semantic stability requires cultural consistency. In brief, words work because people continue to share common ideas, and because both are ultimately grounded in a common psychic and spiritual reality. If the homogeneity of this metaphysical matrix is somehow disturbed and thereby fragmented and impaired, there can be no central and common mentality, no viable *consensus gentium* uniting its members and, therefore, no common language. To whatever degree this fragmentation may have progressed, to that same degree will language become confounded, and communication more of a miracle than it ordinarily is. Just such a condition has, of course, debilitated the academic study of *Walden.*

In the West, the outstanding cause for such fragmentation has been a rapid evolution of consciousness and the changes in thinking which have accompanied it. First, a small portion of the population fell out of a participative relation to the world and into a dualism of mind and matter; and in so doing, this rationalized minority, through science and technology, has over time effected seminal changes in the physical circumstances of life. These changes have in turn accelerated, intensified, and extended the minority condition to strategically prominent segments of society. Spreading by waves of change and adaptation, this materialism, for better or worse, has at last become the victimizing condition of the whole culture. This paradigm describes the circumstances and real forces against which Thoreau wages his war of words and ideas.

The vocabulary applied to these conditions has already been presented, along with the formula for undoing the manifold difficulties they generate. The upshot is that, while the demands of life in this world do not change, we do change, so that by a peculiar formula everything becomes infinitized. Life divided by intellectual zero equals *infinity*. A different formula governs perennial thought, where life divided by insight equals the unity of *one*. The existential counterpart of dividing by zero turns into the first weapon of the gods, which is to say, into madness. Relativity and indecision spread into a psychological epidemic. In real life certain adjustments have to be made in interpreting this formulaic incongruity between life and materialized consciousness, because only the smallest portion of any society are capable of breathing de-animated air for any length of time. Most people want and need flesh-and-blood life. Accordingly, the victimized majority gasp for air, but (unable to find transcendental books about transcendentalists) suffer because they cannot effectively resist. Even among the rational elite appearances are misleading. Those among them who cannot sustain the drain upon their inherited resources as persons, more often than not, survive by neurosis rather than theosis. Such people get a grainy look and walk about like bags of psychic sand.

But the fact remains that for every one of those who can hold his breath indefinitely there are many more who are unsuited to breathe de-animated air. Anthropologically speaking, the forces set in motion by that first few who materialized their relation to themselves and the world, and who are less affected by the great divorce they have brought about, have caused stress to move down the social scale. The overall results of this impossible situation are as varied in their expression as they are monotonous in their outcome. Those who are thus robbed of a sustaining matrix of beliefs, functional rituals, and organic connection to nature, do the best they can. The culturally denuded try to live without a chest in a heartless world. As Thoreau words it, "They make shift to live merely by conformity, practically like their fathers did, and are in no sense the progenitors of a nobler race of men."

Survival is amateur and tragic and amounts to little more than what Thoreau calls "quiet desperation," and lately, what with the help of the mercenaries of cultural warfare, even desperation is not as quiet as it used to be. People hold their breath as long as they can and try hard to live meaningful lives. But eventually they turn blue in the face and fall into desperate gestures. They plunge into perversion if they are sensual, grow neurotic if they are anxious, found new religions if they are silly, take up social causes if they are intellectual, clamor after power if they are political, or they just drop out, noisily if they are young and quietly if they are older.

But as morbidly fascinating as cultural deliquescence may be, its effect upon communication is most important for understanding what Thoreau is trying to reverse in *Walden*. The most important feature of a decomposing culture is the loss of a common, cohesive mentality it brings about. Communication cannot take place among utterly idiosyncratic minds. Such conditions neuter human beings into abstractions of themselves, things called persons, and it is increasingly clear that such spiritually spayed creatures are incapable of sustaining culture even biologically. Thoreau faces the problem of communicating to such isolated egos, asking "Could a greater miracle take place than for us to look through each other's eyes for an instant?" "Perhaps the facts most astounding and most real are never communicated by man to man." Thoreau is willing to take risks and does not care, as he tells us, "how obscene my *words* are," as long as they get the message across. His often overlooked statement that "to act collectively is according to the spirit of our institutions" points to his understanding of the "*com-munity*" communication requires.

As far as thinking goes, which is never further than its delimiting quality, the reasoning and logic each person uses (until logic itself is lost) becomes semantically unstable and ends as a private language. Since semantic stability is based upon a deeper, ritually perpetuated congruity of consciousness, words become loosened from their existential anchors, and everyone begins to speak an idiolect or, as the situation worsens, no language at all. The speaker's meaning, as Owen Barfield puts it, and lexical meaning drift further and further apart until the silver extension cord snaps, the radio goes dead, and the lights go out.

Thoreau seems to have anticipated the fragmentation of language into technological jargon and the effect this has upon communication. He anticipates the down-side of the Internet, where floods of trivial information obviate communication, when he observes that "our inventions ... are but improved means to an unimproved end." In one way or another he is forever reminding us that "the cost of a thing is the amount of what I will call life which is required to be exchanged for it." In this sense very few inventions are unquestionably cost effective, such as the trains, since "if some have the pleasure of riding on a rail, others have the misfortune to be ridden upon." It has taken us a long time to catch up with Thoreau and to realize with C. S. Lewis that "each new power won *by* man is a power *over* man as well."

Although Thoreau speaks in terms of an earlier technology, his criticism remains valid. "We are in great haste," he comments, "to construct a magnetic telegraph from Maine to Texas; but Maine and Texas, it may be, have nothing important to communicate." Today the international news that is beamed by satellite "into the broad, flapping American ear" in ever greater quantities has gained little in quality. As with trains, somehow the energies spent in developing technology have a materializing effect and undermine its original purpose, especially in the case of improvements in the technology of communication. In a very Thoreavian vein Owen Barfield has recently reminded us that:

> It is not much use having a perfect means of communication if you have nothing to communicate except the relative position of bodies in space—or if you will never have anything *new* to communicate. In the same way it is not much use expressing yourself very fully and perfectly indeed—if nobody can understand a word you are saying.

To borrow Jung's words again, "we have reached the limit of our evolution," because perpetually more of the same kind of consciousness is ultimately less. The Internet has not refined humanity.

To be sure, under the moon change is constant. Thoreau reminds us that "all change is a miracle to contemplate; but it is a miracle which is taking place every instant." But although all things change, normal change, including the creeping fallibility of human institutions and the myriad small frictions encumbering their transmission, moves at a reasonable pace. Cultural change is a slow, gradual process, and not altogether unarrestable. But an insidiously terminal kind of change comes about when intellect, breaking into self-consciousness, usurps and partitions the whole kingdom of mind and thereby brings about a radical dislocation within individuals, and between individuals, themselves, and the world. In such terminal anarchy, the abbreviations *BC* and *AD* lose their descriptive value, and *BM* and *AM*, "Before and After Materialism," seem the more appropriate. As scholars who do not buy the basket called Christianity would have it, humanity has entered a very *CE* or "Common Era" indeed. By the time Thoreau comes upon the scene, this state of affairs was well advanced. If Thoreau and his audience had lived in the same world, sharing like beliefs, expectations, values, and so on, then he would have had neither reason nor occasion, nor paradoxically the difficulty, in producing his book. The world would have had to do without its transcendental Gulliver.

On the other hand, although community provides us with words that work, it also has the effect of leaving us without much to say, since within one culture facts tend to be of one kind. Needless to say, *what kind* becomes a question of paramount importance. Within one culture people can speak their own language, and among them the failure to communicate is a matter of relative lucidity. Things may be said well or poorly, but it is hard to say genuinely new things. If Thoreau, therefore, had a great deal in common with his neighbors, either New England would truly have been a lower heaven, or Thoreau, but one among other flinty Yankees. In any case, within one worldview and its complementary culture, profound misunderstandings do not ordinarily arise, and those that do involve degree and complexity rather than kind.

Just the same, in discussing the effects of cultural fragmentation upon language, we must again be careful to distinguish ordinary mistakes within and between worldviews from errors brought about by knowledge that is more than rational. Categorical "biblical" (Philippians 4:7) wisdom that *passeth all understanding* differs from the confusion among understandings. Within a plurality of idiosyncratic minds not one mind may share a common mentality. Although such isolated minds may intersect by accident, generating much ecumenical excitement and certain disillusionment, one cannot be said to include or coincide with another as branches of a tree from a single root. Any sameness that might occur among them is necessarily momentary and fortuitous, existing at one point only and then but for an instant. The problem of communication remains much the same, insofar as we must surmount the self-erected barriers between subjectively isolated minds. And the effort required to do this continues to be "a labor to task the faculties of a man, —such problems ... as demand a universal knowledge." The embarrassingly obvious frequency of talking at cross purposes among undeniably clever people is proof enough that widespread pluralism has displaced the older *consensus gentium,* whether we are considering the world, one culture, or an individual.

But how do we, in fact, cross mental borders into the country of another mind? What kind of a passport do we need? Thoreau asks this very question, "But how to come out of this condition and actually migrate thither?" It is exactly at this point in the grand and only argument, that the differences between English romanticism and American transcendentalism become most pronounced. Coleridge in his *Biographia Literaria* retreats; Thoreau continues to attack. Just as Coleridge is about to provide his pivotal answer, he pretends that a friend to whom he had sent the crucial chapter on "ideal Realism" has written a letter back, advising him not to print it. The letter beginning "Dear C.," warns him that his ideas are too new, reverse everything, and will prove too much for people "to whose unprepared minds your speculations on the esemplastic power would

81

be utterly unintelligible." Thoreau follows a very different, more confident, and adventurous strategy.

Thoreau issues the necessary *epistemological passport*. Few people have applied for one, and fewer have used it for the kind of travelling Thoreau has in mind. But at this crucial juncture he does not let anyone off the hook. He knows that "only the defeated and deserters go to [actual] wars," but he makes sure that even the "cowards that run away and enlist" do not leave his field "without finding the skewer." The more clever among us, of course, avoid this moment of truth by appealing to the mystery of what Thoreau would communicate and proceeding no further. Some can, we say, and some cannot fathom things transcendental. Some are able to migrate thither, some are unable; while others might be able to come out of this condition of fragmented consensus, but choose not to, because they have bought land or cattle or have married. Thoreau will have none of this existential equivocation. He would not have us joining those who practice their religion like "*agri*-culture" and have "*somewhat hastily,* concluded that it is the chief end of man here to 'glorify God and enjoy him forever'." He will agree to no such evasive collusion. There are alternative routes, practical steps to be taken, and more than one check-point on the vast border between here and there.

We can take the Buddha route, Thoreau reminds us, and exercise our private passport to heaven, proceeding directly and collecting all those things thus put under us. But if we take this route, we will have failed at communicating, which does seem to be the chief end of writing, if not of living. Or we can take the Bodhisattva route and postpone nirvana in order to help all beings attain ultimate enlightenment. In this way, we can make better use of this more important lower heaven of language where readers live. Actually, real mystery of the biblical kind is in some ways almost too easy, and mere mystification even easier. But we should avoid hasty appeals to profundity, because on all levels of manifest reality, from atoms to galaxies, "The intellect is a cleaver; it discerns and rifts its way into the secret of things." Even the most divinely besotted Persian admits that many a knot can be "unravel'd by the road" on the way to the "Throne of Saturn."

The intellect should, therefore, be put to good use, in ordering both linguistic possibilities and life's inevitabilities. There is no need to cancel the world in a premature appeal to devotion, morality, or mystery. Heaven is populated neither by benign morons nor by evil geniuses. Before we find ourselves obliged to give up on experience, much useful information can be communicated about reality on this side of the Godhead, if "not the Master-knot of Human Fate." In forgetting that there is an economics of the ethereal as well as the material, people fall into a boom or bust cycle and invent more or less mystery than they need or actually encounter, because "the imagination, give it the least license, dives deeper and soars higher than Nature goes."

How high we can ascend in our understanding of things before major internal adjustments become necessary varies individually, but the writer must consider this question in order to reach the reader. For if communication is to take place between two isolated minds, change must occur. If the greater miracle of moving from one private consciousness to another is to occur, we must accommodate our neighbor, since facts are as inseparable from the qualities of our mind as from another's. Facts as relations between a mind and its world, moreover, are like shadows, insofar as they depend upon the angle of the subjective sun and last only as long as it is shining. To the degree, therefore, that our existence is a complex synonym of our consciousness, then, to that degree we must become what we would say. In spatial language, we must rise to a higher angle of vision from which alone can a new world be seen and expressed.

As Thoreau suggests, the reflections in Walden Pond are in fact a new world, "equally bright" especially when "you invert your head."

In real life we should expect to run into many natural obstructions to such communicative transmigration. In turning our mind inside out and leaping from self to self, we would hardly want to surrender a more or less working model for one of unknown reliability. And we know very well that the unknown goes hand-in-hand with the head, no matter how it joins the shoulders. Consequently, under a fog of religiosity, emotions come crowding in with whispers that this is all easier said than done. But appeals to difficulty as well as to mystery are red herrings not found in *Walden* waters. The difficulty of doing what we know we should do is not the same as the difficulty of knowing what we should do. Apprehension of difficulty is another form of evasion.

Nonetheless, if we would grow in spirit, we must comply with the extra-personal nature of reality, which is "as remote from myself as from another," just as we must eat well if we would grow in body. There is no level of life, this side of the "Master-knot of Human Fate" that cannot be known and understood, and in this sense comprehended systematically according to those qualities proper to it. The size of things is relative. Whether or not an experience is larger than an individual and, therefore, numinous and beyond control depends upon the size of the individual. Maturing individuals, sharing an expanding horizon with other growing gods, do not live less, because what is ordinarily taken to be life has less power over them. There is always "more day to dawn," and some people even overcome their fear of the dark! Change must occur. Thoreau would have us stop "denying the possibility of change" and realize afresh that "all change is a miracle to contemplate; but it is a miracle which is taking place every instant."

Now, in terms of *communication as change*, which is what

LINDISFARNE BOOKS

Lindisfarne Books publishes works of new science, psychology, religion, literature, metaphysics, and spirituality. If you would like a catalog and/or information, please check the appropriate boxes, fill in your name and address, and return this card.

SPECIAL INTERESTS:

☐ Art/Literature (ART)
☐ Celtic (CELT)

☐ Russian Philosophy (RUSS)
☐ Science/Nature (SCIE)
☐ Psychology (MEPSY)

☐ Social Transformation (SOC)
☐ Spiritual Development (INDEV)

This card was found in title...

NAME..

ADDRESS...

CITY...STATE.....................ZIP...........................

COUNTRY...PHONE..

COMMENTS......................................E-MAIL...

....

....

☐ Please send a current catalog

LINDISFARNE BOOKS

3390 Route 9

Hudson, NY 12534-9420 USA

Thoreau is insisting upon, when what is to be communicated is something new and more than routine information of the same kind, a question remains how necessary change does occur. How do we put an end to business as usual at the interminable "Middlesex Cattle Show," which "goes off here with *éclat* annually, as if all the joints of the agricultural machine were suent." If we continue to indulge the petty idealism of the Junior Chamber of Commerce, how can we discover that we are still wearing Lockean glasses and seeing the world in a cross-eyed way? Individual change occurs, of course, whenever we truly want it to happen. The means of change arise because our desire opens an alternative geography of the world. Whatever happens must happen somewhere, somehow, in a body that fits. The concrete question is how?

Thoreau now puns on the French *point d'appui*, for it is at this point that people cast about to prop up their arguments. Here we encounter the leap of illogic. His "attention being wholly occupied with the jump," Thoreau develops this double-edged image as a working metaphor, not only for "throw[ing] one arch over the darker gulf of ignorance" but also for skirting, as opposed to surmounting, life's problems. He extends this metaphor with, "I desire to speak somewhere *without* bounds," which is to say, to speak without limitations and without the slightest leap of illogic. Most philosophers are not as clever as Odysseus in sailing through the Symplegades. They get as far as the crashing cliffs of action and then excuse themselves with theoretical chatter. As Owen Barfield also observes about popularly inadmissible possibilities, "When people start thinking about some topic or other, the near prospect that their train of reasoning may be leading to a conclusion which will infringe the tabu causes them to stop reasoning and make a jump of some sort.... At a certain point fantastic leaps are made." But knowing that "my head is hands and feet," Thoreau would avoid all such fancy philosophical footwork cum sleight of hand. The long and short of it is that you must know what you are about, which is to say, that, first of all, you are in fact about it. Otherwise, "the greatest genuine leap" of self-deception is "to come to earth again."

Coleridge the romantic retreated, apparently because he felt he could not overcome cultural gravity nor successfully compete, therefore, with the fabulous intellectual leaping of wandering Lockeans. The climate of opinion was too strong for him; and so he voluntarily suppressed his chapter on "*ideal Realism.*" Thoreau the transcendentalist presses his attack and charges that the number of philosophical "cowards that run away and enlist" in the ranks of rationalists is very large. Sidestepping the challenge is easier than taking an unutterable stand. Jonathan Swift enlisted with satire; Hawthorne joined up with abortive romance; Kierkegaard signed-on with irony, and so on. People who think like Aristotle and claim they have never leapt are leaping all the time. Plato's gang toe the line, admit their vaulting, and overcome the gravity of their readers. Thoreau joins them with:

> In any weather, at any hour of the day or night, I have been anxious to improve the nick of time, and notch it on my stick too; to stand on the meeting of two eternities, the past and future, which is precisely the present moment; to toe that line. You will pardon some obscurities, for there are more secrets in my trade than in most men's, and yet not voluntarily kept, but inseparable from its very nature. I would gladly tell all that I know about it, and never paint "No Admittance" on my gate.

Thoreau would tell all, even more than religious teachers from the Near East.

To avoid begging the question, Thoreau's co-authors are obliged to set one intellectual foot upon their intuition and the other upon the perennial tradition as it is found in the "Scriptures of the nations" and the "Bibles of mankind." There the "hard bottom and rocks in place" and the enabling interrelatedness of things is found. Communication is possible, in the last analysis, because all things *are grounded on the same basis and, therefore, truly related.* From a sufficiently subtle point of view, all things are the same one thing. Communication happens, because one thing may thus coincide with another. In other words, when we are ready, we can change and through ourselves enter into this one fact. All great traditions hold to the perennial doctrine of the one and the many, in which every grain of sand contains the universe in small. Thoreau confirms this Emersonian version of the sameness in difference. He was convinced that "if we knew all the laws of Nature, we should need only one fact, or the description of one actual phenomenon, to infer all the particular results at that point."

Change as the means and substance of communicating among apparently exclusive conditions, as these take flesh in people, is in the last analysis possible, because nothing is or can be absolutely isolated. Many people accept this one fact abstractly, yet never apply it to themselves. Rather, they limit it to what they understand to be matter. Those who deny it outright do so with a contradictory materialism, since the language they use implies the very thing they deny. But like the ponds in Thoreau's lake country, all things are really "so much alike that you would say they must be connected under ground." Communication, thus, amounts to bringing such underground connections into the light of day in new times and spaces. Comprehending this universal interrelatedness is always an ontological problem before it becomes an epistemological error. But experiencing interrelatedness remains the only solvent for the sin of separateness. Thoreau suggests a biblical test (Matthew 5:45): "We might try our lives by a thousand simple tests; as, for an instance, that the same sun which ripens my beans illumines at once a system of earth like ours."

In insisting upon this crucial point, Thoreau is fully aware that he has entered the theological arena of grace, and once more he obliges his co-authors to do the same. He compels us to acknowledge that everything turns on our definition of our own so-called natural powers. If these do not encompass the *capacity to change*, then grace becomes a logical necessity, the tertium quid, or third thing, required to connect absolute God and relative humanity. If we decide we are incapable of change, then communication through the organic motion of change becomes a delusion, and Thoreau leaps no closer to heaven than his "wandering Arabs" who always "come to earth again." If we cannot change ourselves, then, another good book like Walden is just another exercise in mental acrobatics that never gets off the ground. Without an ear for change we could not hear "the writer [who] speaks to the intellect and heart of mankind, to all in any age who can *understand* him." Thoreau, however, is convinced that our "capacities have never been measured."

Yet we forget that the pivotal question of grace is in the end autobiographical, because "we commonly do not remember that it is, after all, always the first person that is speaking." And this first of all persons is the Spectator (Sanskrit *sākshin*), the one and only transmigrant described by Thoreau as "a part of me, which, as it were, is not a part of me, but spectator ... no more I than it is you." But we can change, because "We are all sculptors and painters, and our material is our own flesh and blood and bones."

Thoreau, however, outdoes even his fourth-century comrade at arms Pelagius in attacking original sin and affirming our freedom to shape our own righteous destiny.

Thoreau aims at nothing less than "to carve and paint the very atmosphere and medium through which we look, which morally we can do." By supplying the means as well as the capacity for human change, he would solve all "the problems of life, not only theoretically, but practically." A rigidly negative view of human nature overlooks the fact that better theologians would come up with better theologies, since our powers improve as we grow closer to God. In pointing to the "paths which the mind travels," Thoreau is optimistic about our prospects and reminds us, "that if one advances confidently in the direction of his dreams, and endeavors to live the life which he has imagined, he will meet with a success unexpected in common hours."

He assures us first that we are wrong when "we think that we can change our clothes only," and then goes on to remind us that we are more deeply wrong if we persist in "denying the possibility of change. This is the only way, we say; but there are as many ways as there can be drawn radii from one centre. All change is a miracle to contemplate; but it is a miracle which is taking place every instant." Again and again Thoreau forces us to remember who is speaking and that the voice we hear is our own. We must define ourselves before we can discuss our capacity to change. The lexicographer who opts for a low definition of human nature, because the circle of "scholar-like thoughts" assumes that "man's capacities have [indeed] been measured," becomes "but the slave and prisoner of his own opinion of himself." Turning to the Scriptures of the nations in order to drive his point home in as many ways as he can, Thoreau draws specifically upon the Vedic idea of *dharma*. If we do our proper duty, we will succeed in changing for the better. The real first person says "I love to weigh, to settle, to gravitate toward that which most strongly and rightfully attracts me ... not [to] suppose a case, but take the case that is; to travel the only path I can, and that on which no power can resist me."

Thoreau is not being anti-Christian here; he is only being anti-Augustinian, which is quite different. He is asking no more than that we use our free will, of which the saint had a rather low opinion. There is no contradiction here, not if we take *I*, that is, *us*, in the largest possible sense. But if we leap over this point on the wrong foot, taking *I* to refer merely to a reasoning animal, then we will very quickly "come to earth again" and land in great muck and confusion about "fate, free will, [and] foreknowledge absolute." Thoreau's *I* does not name our lower, merely psychological personality, but our true individuality as spiritual beings who are not separate from Christ the Logos. By definition, the creaturely *I* that the materialist calls natural man can neither remain in nor re-enter the lower heaven of paradise. We need only to try ourselves by another simple test and rephrase the biblical question Who told us we were only natural? The answer is ourselves. The Spectator is the sameness which communicates. The same Son shines in and on all of us.

Considerable thought and earnest endeavor, however, are required to comprehend the truth that order is never merely private, and that there are orders upon orders, compounded of orders, hierarchies of compounded orders, and so on up the ladder until "all the chinks in the scale of being are filled." "The sun is but a morning star." One or even many orders may dissolve into a lower, preceding order, as our sophisticated civilizations may slip periodically into sanative barbarism. The biological disorder of decomposition depends upon chemical order. There is always something left: nature remains, or a dead nature, or just matter and atoms, or just laws of physics operating upon a plenum of primitive stringy energy, or just space, or no space, and so on down the ladder.

The eighteenth-century complacency of Alexander Pope may irritate those people who hunt platitudes rather than windmills; but he was not wrong when he restated the principle that chaos is order misunderstood. Of course, some orders are more friendly than others, to human beings, and their absence may be regarded as chaos. Yet *friendly* is relative and nothing to build a religion on. Friendly religion leaps blind and backward into the aesthetic world of mere taste, which, if not to be disputed, is still nothing to the point. As far as leaping goes, it is better to jump at knowledge than to remain on earth in boundless ignorance.

In actuality we learn over and over that squabbling about such questions as these arises from what men and women are, which is to say, what they have already made themselves into, and this ordinarily precedes what they now think. When men and women make themselves into persons, they naturally desire to be free and to have their liberty to do anything they want, right or wrong. When sufficient numbers of persons accumulate and agree on this point, they cause a Renaissance. But personal freedom, as it is still commonly perpetrated, is forever in danger of degenerating into a dream of perpetual postponement. For time passes, and delusions flourish like "haughty weeds." And in spite of our drives and needs, "things do not change; we change," and existential bills come due, since "the cost of a thing is the amount of what I will call life which is required to be exchanged for it, immediately or in the long run."

There must be a happy side to the "many successive falls" humans experience. But when persons come to write books, the cost of life goes up. The derelictions of late industrial civilization foster a priesthood of authors and allow them to occupy cultural offices that demand greater wisdom than they possess. Smaller and smaller persons occupy positions of greater and greater power. In this predicament, as in others, there are as many degrees as there are reasons for acting less responsibly than we ought. But the human cost is the same, the damage as permanent, even though the perpetrators postpone their rewards.

History, as well as intuition and scripture, corroborates change as the basis of communication. Even history, however, cannot escape the Procrustean measure of the felt validity of the evidence adduced. Although we might adduce many things that fit "you who read these pages ... something about your condition," reason would be found to reject the same thing as not the same thing. In a word, the very condition toward which "the facts, the case that is" might be directed is likely to be used to intercept and depotentiate the attack upon the self we have decided to be and, for the time being, to remain. And like the medieval youths of Kolbek who could not stop dancing, around we would go—the younger the longer.

Nevertheless, the knowledge that interrelated existence supports the mechanisms of psychic change needed to communicate new qualities is ageless and universal. Every great tradition presents philosophical equivalents. From India come the terms *parasparāpeksha* and *parasparasraya*, "perception of one-another" and "connection with one-another," which describe the mutual-relatedness of things. From China comes the fourfold statement: "One is in one: one is in all; all is in one; all is in all." Speaking in terms of individuals, Japan's twelfth-century sage Ryonin says: "One person is all persons; all persons are one person." And closer to home, in the fifteenth century, Nicholas of Cusa writes:

> A certain infinity belongs ... to each individual thing, in the sense that in the characteristics of its essence it carries within itself also the characteristics of all other individuals. All is in all; *omnia ubique*. In this way every individual contains within itself the universe, though in a limited form peculiar to this individual alone and differing from all others. Each individual thus is, if rightly and fully known, a mirror of the universe.

Emerson was fond of reiterating such truths as these. The number of quotations from the Scriptures of the nations might be multiplied almost indefinitely, to little, no, or every effect. Their final and chief communicative impact, surprisingly, might first be emotional, on the chance that the cumulative force of such a barrage might be just enough to embarrass certain types of persons into a moment or two of awareness. For after all, how many traditions can a person dismiss in the face of centuries of concurrent and unvaried testimony! Historical comparisons might at least get a personality into church, where it might become a man or a woman to learn that our "discoveries were not by the synthetic but analytic process."

Perhaps falls are felicitous. In the periodic desanctifying of the world, which has comprised so much of recent history, intensely material moments have been accompanied by equally intense self-consciousness. Surveying the "world through a telescope or a microscope, and never with [the] natural eye," we have not remembered Emerson's example, which is to make a macroscope of that magic lens, equipped as it is with its own mind-piece, and to use it for looking into the one reality lying in other directions. Coleridge retreated before the huge momentum of his contemporaries' opaque certainties. He felt it was impossible (in so many words and without recondite circumlocution) to "say what you have to say, not what you ought." As a result, the letter he wrote to himself gave way to another "what you ought" and never got off the ground. His leap had to wait. But in a Blakean way, the road back to wisdom, if not to Xanadu, has been through the very excess of mechanoscopic scientism that canceled Coleridge's communication.

But Intellect the Cleaver, like Odin's magic auger Rati, has penetrated too far, now, for us to arrest its progress. We cannot stop now and homestead where we are on the cosmic mountain, not without paying a terrible price for our willful opacities. In every direction we look, the solid world of dead matter is disappearing into the smartest and most vital molecules one could ever hope to meet, full of brains, energy, and the capacity to change. If molecules can mutate, why should we assume we cannot? Before our very eyes the residual phenomenon changes into the volatile noumenon. Chemicals and viruses exchange places; molecules and ideas become indistinguishable. Language and perception retreat into mind, as entire pantheons of modern idols grow ghostly and become "instantly *translated*." The single lesson of the sciences themselves, and of biology and physics in particular, rehearses the marvelous reciprocity of mind and object. Our too solid flesh has indeed begun to melt. These are not romantic dreams, but transcendental realities. The time for strategic vagueness has passed, and the notorious *we* have lost all our excuses.

The upshot of all this is that once again, for a while, we can reverse Coleridge's retreat. We can find the central post office and reclaim his lost letter before history closes. If we remember the Word that writes all letters, we can now write our own letters to the world, which, in uttering more unutterable things, will communicate metaphysics to materialists. Like a rainbow in an afternoon sun the spectral interrelatedness of all things has become newly visible—if not through a sunset shower, then through tears at night.

7

MEANWHILE THOREAU'S BEANS

Yankee Samsāra[1]

Beans mean Pythagoras. But few people have figured out what the philosopher means by his famous rule against eating them, not to mention Thoreau's decision to break it, in spite of the fact he was "by nature a Pythagorean." The answer to this mysterious prohibition lies in the *Veda* and in ancient zoological mythology from around the world. Today, we would have to listen for it in nursery tales and Mother Goose rhymes. To communicate essentials, what is it but to put Humpty Dumpty back together again! To live, to die in order to live, what is it but *to eat beans*?

Prenatal humanity, swimming blissfully in the immaterial womb of Mother Nature, knew this world was alive—a giant, essentially friendly creature, in whom they lived, moved, and began to have their biological being, and whom later they would happily dismember and continue to dismember, in order to have their world as well. The memory of this collective childhood found one expression in the experience of the universe as a divine, sacrificial animal and, more narrowly, in the conviction that the sun is this divine "bull's" eye. What to us are merely astronomical phenomena, such as an eclipse or even the alternation of day and night, were

---

1. The transitory world of endless birth and death.

to our more participative ancestors the actions of giant animals. In the Mother Goose rhyme, the "cow" jumps over the
"moon," which is the "bean" the solar "cow" finds and eats,
at sunrise. In the nursery tale, Jack sells this divine "cow" for
magic "beans," because the only way out of the world is to
climb over the moon on the "beanstalk" of time. The folk
message is clear: eternity is experienced through time,
whether it is called *samsāra* or the fall.

Thoreau has earlier expressed the paradox of time and
eternity in the language of fishing and digging. He tells us
that "time is but the stream I go a-fishing in," but because his
"head is an organ for burrowing," to "fish in the sky" is to
"mine and burrow my way through these hills." Now, in
keeping with the major positive turn into *Walden*'s second
group of six chapters, he turns to a more visceral level of
experience through images of food and eating. "It is a vulgar
error," he says, "to suppose that you have tasted huckleberries who never plucked them." And "whetted by experience," he confesses that he did both at Walden: "I might add
eating, for I did taste." Passing over what St. Paul has to say
on what is permitted to the holy, he supports his point by cit-
ing the *Veda* to the effect that "'he who has true faith in the
Omnipresent Supreme Being may eat all that exists'."

Thoreau dines in his own transcendental fashion, in
which eating can be a source of genuine inspiration: "Who
has not sometime derived an inexpressible satisfaction
from his food in which appetite had no share? I have been
thrilled to think that I owed a mental perception to the
commonly gross sense of taste, that I have been inspired
through the palate, that some berries which I had eaten on
a hillside had fed my genius." Mythologically speaking, to
eat berries or beans is to eat the moon, and thus to taste of
time, life, and death. Change is the rule in this sublunary
world, for the Moon is also Lucina, the changeable Goddess of Childbirth, as well as the cool virgin Diana.

96

Thoreau's mythological virtuosity, "being liquid and ample" like Walden Pond, has been more than enough to fill volumes of second-water "scholar-like thoughts." The fabric of allusions opening "The Bean-Field" alone would fill many chapters in its unraveling. Why "seven miles," and later "twelve bushels"? Why the puns on "pulse" as "beans" and "throb" of life, and the "fine broad leaf to look on" as "beans" and as "*Walden*"? Obviously Thoreau knows his beans. Earlier in *Walden* he has already prepared the field where he cultivates them, by describing its mental counterpart in "Solitude" as "a human entity; the scene, so to speak, of thoughts and affections." The field of human endeavor is our own flesh and blood, and it is "labor enough to subdue and cultivate a few cubic feet of flesh." "We are all sculptors and painters, and our material is our own flesh and blood and bones." The questions Thoreau asks in the paragraph opening "The Bean-Field" also signal a major outward turn which complements the inward settling and wedging "through the mud and slush of opinion" in the first six chapters.

So *Walden*'s first major turn occurs between the sixth chapter, "Visitors," and the seventh chapter, "The Bean-Field." Evidence of this node in the growth of Thoreau's book lies primarily in his shift from inner to outer concerns. His inquiry into timeless realities is applied to well-timed actualities, as he moves from mind and self to nature and society. What could be more timely, therefore, than Thoreau's cultivation of Pythagoras and of beans, the very symbol of our vegetable-like mutability?

A summary comparison of chapter titles will bring out the movement of Thoreau's thought by highlighting differences in subject and point of view. In sum, the first six chapters are largely introspective in character and move from "the grossest groceries" to "the finest sediment." The next six chapters, though dusted with "the bloom of the present moment" of earlier chapters, are ethical and objective, and move from "beans" to "brutes." This larger complementary relationship asserts itself in many ways. Philosophical "Economy," for example, complements the bodily "Bean-Field." "Where I Lived, and What I Lived For" describes a life more ethereal than that lived in "The Village." "Reading" is limited to books but "The Ponds" opens the book of nature. One hears distant "Sounds" but goes to "Baker Farm." "Solitude" is private but "Higher Laws" is Mosaic and public. Most striking, perhaps, is the contrast between the respective concluding chapters, in which "Visitors" come from heaven but "Brute Neighbors" live next door!

Thoreau is representatively Western in his general opposition of *inner* and *outer* and his use of this dichotomy as an expression of things timeless and time bound. Spatial language never ceases to be a key vehicle for his dialectic and its complementary levels of mind and experience. His reanimation of space into something much more intimate and alive than three empty dimensions remains one of the major structural features of his book. Always implicit, it is here elevated and enlarged into the means and reason for a major turn in his thought. Within *Walden*'s strenuous spatial idiom, *in* and *out* encompass a dualism of immense living importance. Even though space is not always labeled with obvious prepositions, it remains the constant fulcrum for the interplay of literal and figurative senses in his language. A parallel psychologizing of motion is also at work within Thoreau's language and ideas. His thought and language etherealize material forms into meaning, and the resultant movement—from things, through words, into ideas, and on into transcendental experience—becomes another confirmation of the living changes upon which communication depends. Always, the "residual statement" soars into corresponding "volatile truth," which is but another way of saying that the outer world gives rise to an inner world of higher truth. In plain language, everything has a meaning.

This transformation of things and bodies into thought-forms is implicit in earlier chapters long before Thoreau uses it to mark this major division between the first two groups of chapters. In "Economy," for example, he reports that "in those days, when my hands were much employed, I read but little." At the close of his second chapter "Where I Lived, and What I lived For," expressing his desire not "to be any more busy with my hands than is necessary," he tells us further that "my head is hands and feet." And then again in "Reading," he confesses that "I kept Homer's *Iliad* on my table through the summer, though I looked at his page only now and then. Incessant labor with my hands, at first, for I had my house to finish and my beans to hoe at the same time, made more study impossible."

The point at hand is the way Thoreau works toward his central spatial idiom, and the light this sheds on the way his thought informs his language. But we should not overlook the way his language at the same time never ceases to imply an answering unity in life, a "connecting link between wild and cultivated fields," and thus to reveal still other means of communication. Here the words *at his page* transform what is outwardly a bean-field into Thoreau's equally Homeric and timeless page of the world, where he in fact did live and work at making the world say beans. Although the phrase *at first* implies that differences between manual and mental labor were quickly transcended, the word *more* confirms that Homering, hammering, and hoeing are all forms of *study*. While the full passage develops, contrasts, and matches inner questions with outer answers, the blending of manual with mental labor and the grounding of both in their spiritual equivalences anticipate the development of later chapters.

On the most basic level, the very first phrase of *Walden's* second group of chapters, "MEANWHILE my beans," returns the reader, with rare figurative husbandry, to Thoreau's "actual history" at the pond. As he brings into focus his several leguminous references earlier scattered in seminal passages, we see him at work beside the pond. The predicate of the complex opening sentence, "were impatient to be hoed," not only further defines his goal but also cultivates a new understanding of its earlier expressions. In "Solitude" Thoreau tells us that we can be "beside ourselves in a sane sense." "However intense my experience," he reports, "I am conscious of the presence and criticism of a ... spectator." And now hoeing beans recalls and thematically enlarges such philosophical statements with actual experience, for now "It was no longer beans that I hoed, nor I that hoed beans."

Looking toward divine impartiality, such language first expands literal cultivation into a figurative and then into a symbolic activity. In "Economy," people are cultivated for their roots, not their flowers, and they "find it labor enough to subdue and cultivate a few cubic feet of flesh," while their "better part ... is soon plowed into the soil for compost." A close look at the thematic metaphors running throughout *Walden*—in this instance the image of cultivation as etherealization—consistently shows how Thoreau's thought is connected to his words, and his words to his deeds, according to the implicit transcendental priorities he later spells out in so many words in his "Conclusion." Throughout *Walden* the world is "elastic," theory is practice, movement is change, transitions are always transformations, and every message the same communication.

This we can see if we pick up our hoe and follow Thoreau to the bean field. Out of his labors at cultivation he harvests those literal and figurative connections that tie "The Bean-Field" to its sequel "The Village." And in this way he comes to serve as his own "parable-maker," as he garners the "classic result" of an "instant and immeasurable crop" of immense and ineffable self-knowledge. His identification of self-cultivation and the cultivation of beans, as we have seen, recalls the Spectator in "Solitude," "that is no more I than it is you." But it is squarely upon the foundation of self-knowledge that Thoreau proceeds to build his transpersonal participation in nature. He assures us that "if you have built castles in the air, your work need not be lost; that is where they should be. Now put the foundations under them." To this project he adds an element of time and, thus, a serial view of cultivation as personal maturation and general evolution. It was as a child "four years old" that the precocious Thoreau first saw the field where he would later grow beans. Then and now this field was "that fabulous landscape of my infant dreams" where, assisting one articulation of the very Logos, he makes the "earth say beans instead of grass," and where later, "digging one day for fishworms, I discovered the ground-nut (*Apios tuberosa*) on its string, the potato of the aborigines, a sort of fabulous fruit, which I had begun to doubt if I had ever dug and eaten in childhood, as I had told, and had not dreamed it."

Transcendental experiences are not romantic dreams; they have foundations. And we are urged more than once to consider "what foundation a door, a window, a cellar, a garret, have in the nature of man." Although Thoreau now finds himself obliged to make "invidious distinctions" between beans and other weeds, he remembers that "we are wont to forget that the sun looks on our cultivated fields and on the prairies and forests without distinction. They all reflect and absorb his rays alike, and the former make but a small part of the glorious picture which he beholds in his daily course. In his view the earth is all equally cultivated like a garden." And in this garden we humans are not necessarily the only and "principal cultivator," or cultivar.

The impartiality of this view connects "The Bean-Field" to "The Village," which Thoreau then "looks on" "in his view" as if it were just another of the myriad weeds sown upon the earth. In fact, the first words of this next chapter echo the opening phrase of "The Bean-Field." "After hoeing" resonates with "MEANWHILE my beans," and the context of impartial observation it has established. "The Bean-Field," thus, not only begins the second, central section of *Walden* with a positive return to the world but it also defines the nature of this return and kind of connections we should expect throughout the second group of six chapters.

Recalling, then, the *equivalence* among hoeing beans, self-cultivation, and studying, the reader is prepared to taste and to be inspired by heeding the spiritual equivalences suggested by such phrases as "After hoeing, or perhaps reading and writing," in which three verbs identify one activity. "Some must work in fields if only for the sake of tropes and expression," since these are the *fishworms* used in catching the minds of men. And by recalling the spiritual geography of *inner* and *outer,* implied by "In one direction ... in the other horizon," one can chart "whole new continents and worlds within you." Indeed, the whole passage deserves recollection: "In one direction from my house there was a colony of muskrats in the river meadows; under the grove of elms and buttonwoods in the other horizon was a village of busy men, as curious to me as if they had been prairie-dogs, each sitting at the mouth of its burrow, or running over to a neighbor's to gossip." Since the sun shines "on the prairies and forests without distinction," and men should not be too "busy with their beans," Thoreau's humor is somewhat more than obvious, especially if we heed the next sentence: "I went there frequently to observe their habits." From an eternal point of view—*sub species aeternitatis*—muskrats and men have more in common than either might suspect or wish to admit.

Thoreau's play upon "to observe"—that is, not only *to watch* but also *to take part in*—unites participation and impartial judgment with humility in a fresh and cogent equivalence that connects "The Bean-Field" and "The Village" in still other ways. Gossip in "homeopathic doses" is as bracing and humbling "as the rustle of leaves and the peeping of frogs"; and "birds and squirrels" are as interesting as "men and boys." Concord, as well as Amherst, was a mysterious empire where muskrats played, huckleberries died, and "elms and buttonwoods" bowed to God.

Thoreau's anthropological joke—which actually begins in "Economy" with the "bravery of minks and muskrats"— runs throughout much of "The Village" and is enlivened by his sense of divine equivalence among all creatures. Viewed without selfish bias, the world stands up again into Eden, a garden teeming with miraculous plants, colonies of animals, and villages of humans. The genuine open-mindedness with which Thoreau reports his newly unfallen world is quite opposite to that mental rigidity and low self-opinion with which most observers enslave themselves. His "elastic and vigorous thought" provides a springboard for his imminent leap toward "Baker Farm," where he goes fishing and catches a glistening string of "Higher Laws."

The consistency of this progression alone is enough to unify this second step of Thoreau's communicative strategy, but the virtuosity of his metaphors reaches far beyond their immediate contexts. A concatenation of equivalent differences leads his reader through a second series of transformations connecting chapter to chapter, providing earthly parallels to the philosophical progression of chapters one through six. The movement between "The Village" and "The Ponds" is made both spatially apt and emotionally compelling, as Thoreau adapts the loco-descriptive technique of eighteenth-century landscape poetry to his transcendental purposes. First, although he does not burden us with a "behold," he directs our *inner* and *outer* eye to the fact the ponds are located "farther westward" from the village "in the other horizon." Second, within Thoreau's cosmogonal geography these bodies of water also present a new but equivalent kind of *society*, afforded by the democracy of that universal village called the cosmos. Thoreau, "having had a surfeit of human society and gossip," would turn and try another sort of larger society among other features of the landscape. As he tells us, "Instead of calling on some scholar, I paid many a visit to particular trees." His friendship with the old, deaf fisherman exemplifies the tenor of these other natural acquaintances. Their "intercourse was altogether one of unbroken harmony, far more pleasing to remember than if it had been carried on by speech." With such intimate, silent equality, he undertakes an exploration of the full world—apart from merely human society—and the position of humanity in this world.

"The Village" is followed by "The Ponds," and if any chapter in *Walden* warrants the elevating adjective *central,* "The Ponds" deserves the honor. For in sounding Walden Pond and its liquid relations, the book *Walden* becomes most profoundly metaphysical and self-referential. Here, in the depth of book and pond, the cumulative conditioning of the reader is plumbed with weighted Thoreauvian lines. We are obliged to reorganize our self-estimate by statements like "A lake is the landscape's most beautiful and expressive feature. It is earth's eye; looking into which the beholder measures the depth of his own nature." If our eyes are now open and our minds awake, we will recall that the "landscape" before us as readers is the book *Walden*, which, its author is suggesting, is also a "bottomless pond" wherein we may measure our own depth, looking eye-to-eye with Thoreau or, rather, with the "spectator ... that is no more I than it is you."

The subtle complexity of this chapter, which aligns book, pond, author, reader, human nature, and the universe, points to Thoreau's much abused admonition: "To read well ... will task the reader." Without embarrassment Thoreau is *hard* upon his reader. In this chapter he again takes up the full range of his thematic imagery and, in so doing, compounds its symbolic meaning. As he does with the word *beans*, he displays consummate foresight in his careful planting and cultivating of ideas, so that they blossom in a field of the reader's consciousness where their true beauty and power can flourish. Thoreau is nothing like the flinty farmer "who loves not the beauty of his fruits," but sells them. The fruits carried in the basket called *Walden* "are too pure to have a market value." After an image or theme blossoms, we find its seeds coming up through the later pages of his book. Thoreau's interest in the dispersion of seeds is not limited to field botany but extends to the germs of ideas.

Especially in "The Ponds" do we meet with a harvest of profound equivalences. An apparently casual reference, for example, to a pond or to a well grows into a reminder that this apparently solid and secure earth is "but dry land," a fact of life reflected in the actual fluctuations of Walden Pond, where "fishing goes on again in the meadow." Economic themes, such as mercenary perversion, are resumed in the discussion of Flint's Pond, named for an "unclean and stupid farmer.... who thought only of its money value.... who would carry the landscape, who would carry his God, to market, if he could get anything for him." Solitude and society are taken up again in *Walden*, pond and book, which, of all companions "wears best, and best preserves its purity." A full description of this cross-referential dovetailing and refinement of images and ideas would require its own chapter, and would exceed this brief outline. But within "The Ponds" connections are based upon the character of the ponds themselves. Each pond—Walden, Flint's, Goose, Fair Haven, White—is uniquely and intimately linked, sometimes "under ground": "I have said that Walden has no visible inlet nor outlet, but it is on the one hand distantly and indirectly related to Flint's

Pond ... and on the other directly and manifestly to Concord River"—and, of course, to Thoreau's report of his journey on that river.

The idea of interrelatedness is never absent from the pages of *Walden*. Going beyond another sly comment upon *A Week*, which was his first attempt to say the unsayable, through this neighborhood of ponds Thoreau here describes "my lake country," as he humorously calls it, allegorizing Wordsworth into what the poet might have become if romanticism had not failed, but, as Owen Barfield puts it, had "come of age." Strategically as well as structurally "The Ponds" claims its important place, because it once more refines and advances Thoreau's communicative effort. Summarizing his transcendental limnology, he concludes his survey of the ponds with: "These, with Concord River, are my water privileges; and night and day, year in year out, they grind such grist as I carry to them." If we read too much like the namesake of Flint's Pond, we will find no *privilege* here, where Thoreau reconfirms the subjective nature of experience and once more establishes a foundation for another leap at the truth, this time from the bottom of White Pond: "As at Walden, in sultry dog-day weather, looking down through the woods on some of its bays which are not so deep but that the reflection from the bottom tinges them, its waters are of a misty bluish-green or glaucous color."

Like the ancient Greek philosopher Thales, Thoreau suggests that the whole world is water. His implicit equation of sky and water, his allegory of the *bottom* of things, and references to his leaping fish, comprise another variation upon his communicative parable: the deeper meanings of things are, to the informed eye, visible through their surfaces and, perhaps, only so. Early in "Where I Lived, and What I Lived For," Thoreau describes Walden Pond as "a lower heaven itself so much the more important," precisely for the reason that it can be used as a lens to see higher heaven. In "The

Ponds," repeating this same idea of convex-concave vision, he tells us that "Lying between the earth and the heavens, it partakes of the color of both," because "a field of water … is intermediate in its nature between land and sky." This same chapter closes with an apostrophe to nature which stresses the same communicative importance of that portion of reality we can, to our profit, contact with our senses. The formula remains the same: communication depends upon change and reunification through the realization of deeper identities:

> White Pond and Walden are great crystals on the surface of the earth, Lakes of Light…. How much more beautiful than our lives, how much more transparent than our characters, are they! … Nature has no human inhabitant who appreciates her…. She flourishes most alone, far from the towns where they reside. Talk of heaven! ye disgrace earth.

To undo and recover this insult, Thoreau next moves on to "Baker Farm," where with the seeds of wisdom the barren earth is properly re-graced into Eden.

"Baker Farm" opens with Thoreau rambling among trees "like fleets at sea, full-rigged, with wavy boughs." This nautical metaphor recalls Thoreau's earlier use of sailing imagery in his report of launching himself into the night and setting sail from "The Village."

> It was very pleasant, when I stayed late in town, to launch myself into the night, especially if it was dark and tempestuous, and set sail from some bright village parlor or lecture room … for my snug harbor in the woods, having made all tight without and withdrawn under hatches with a merry crew of thoughts, leaving only my outer man at the helm, or even tying up the helm when it was plain sailing. I had many a genial thought by the cabin fire "as I sailed."

In "House Warming" the inner light of this *cabin fire* is elaborated into "You can always see a face in the fire." The Spectator watches. Stoking his fire with a few piece of "fat pine," Thoreau anticipates his necrology of "Former Inhabitants; and Winter Visitors," remembering "how much of this food for fire is still concealed in the bowels of the earth." But in the present context of "The Ponds" and "Baker Farm," sailing is the foremast food for thought, and we can see how the image carries us from the village to "The Ponds," so that we arrive (down wind of a double pun on "wavy boughs") at "Baker Farm": "Sometimes I rambled to pine groves, standing like temples, or like fleets at sea, full-rigged, with wavy boughs, and rippling with light, so soft and green and shady that the Druids would have forsaken their oaks to worship in them." Thoreau's rambling higher and higher into the country of "Valhalla" leads to trees rather than scholars and connects the sustained image of sailing with his play upon transcendental diversity in "having had a surfeit of human society." In this way, natural features of the landscape, animals, people, whole villages, enter again into a new and social equivalence which facilitates the movement between these two chapters.

The "Baker Farm" adventure with John Field shows how people do "disgrace" this earth and themselves with their "own opinion" of both. The negative powers of projection are another facet of Thoreau's protean theme, and no one is more keenly aware than he that "the universe constantly and obediently answers to our conceptions.... Things do not change; we change." So it is that the dull drab world of this unfortunate old-world Irishman, John Field, describes nothing but his very own shadow, which balances and punctuates the glistening rainbow world of Thoreau, for "darkness reveals the heavenly lights."

The "visible darkness" of John Field's "bogging" world reminds us of how pointedly Miltonic Thoreau's language is.

The opening of "Baker Farm" echoes the technique and substance of the description of Paradise, right down to "nameless other wild forbidden fruits, too fair for mortal taste," and continues into a delightful pun upon the sour Puritan's beechen bowl. Successive comparisons, mounting, wide-reaching eclectic images, and a moral focus upon *forbidden fruits* extend the Pythagorean question of tasting beans and collectively nourish the subtly ironic relevance of invoking the shade of the blind poet in a celebration of a world that still is a glistening paradise. "Instead of calling on some scholar," Thoreau quips, "I paid many a visit to particular trees." We wonder what scholar Thoreau had in mind; but in any case, instead of reading what a particular poet has written *about* paradise, he visits Baker Farm, and gathers fresh fruits even from a "blasted" Wordsworthian tree.

Thoreau's communicative parable continues through a mosaic of images and concludes in his patriarchal return from the heights of "Baker Farm" with his tablet of "Higher Laws," looking like a Yankee-faced Moses back from a place that certainly does not disgrace this earth. From this high, and dry, ground, where "like a dolphin" he showed his back to the world, he wondered "at the halo of light around my shadow" as he returned "through the woods with my string of fish." John Field, hacking away with his "moral bog hoe" and trying to live in a new world by an "old-country mode," was not as lucky. None of us will "rise in this world" until we abandon our "boggy ways." We are fated "to come to earth again" until our "wading webbed bog-trotting feet get *talaria* to their heels." The actual Baker Farm is as much a condition as a place.

Thoreau's concluding apostrophe: "Go fish and hunt far and wide day by day," is taken up again in the next chapter, "Higher Laws," as he elevates fishing and hunting into their spiritual equivalent, the search for truth. Already, in "The Ponds," fish have grown wings and become flying creatures who soar into the depths of Walden Pond, when a human, floating on top of their world, chances to disturb their kingdom slightly more solid than air. Even earlier, men come to Walden Pond to fish more in their own natures than in mere pond water. "Baker Farm" completes this cycle of imagery. The injunction "Remember [now] thy Creator in the days of thy youth" (Ecclesiastes 12:1) is directed at reading "Higher Laws," where, as the chapter progresses, the thought proceeds from youth to maturity, from the crudeness of boyish fishing and hunting to the refinement of grown-up search for truth and true souls. Thoreau, "remembering that it was one of the best parts of my education," develops the admonition: "Go fish and hunt far and wide day by day,—farther and wider" into a second imperative: "*make* them hunters, though sportsmen only at first, if possible, mighty hunters at last, so that they shall not find game large enough for them in this or any vegetable wilderness,—hunters as well as fishers of men." Hunting and fishing thus become a kind of violent apostolic self-cultivation, which yields maturity in another complex expression—and experience—of self-realization.

Since Thoreau has told us that he is drawing upon the "Scriptures of the nations," it should not come as a surprise that biblical parallels are never far in the background in any portion of *Walden*. Here in Thoreau's allegorizing of hunting, I Corinthians 13:11 is the relevant verse: when a boy, Thoreau thought and hunted as a boy; but when a man, he hunts as a man and brings back a new set of commandments. Indeed, this book of the New Testament is especially relevant to Thoreau's communicative designs, in its concern with teaching holy truths to humanity and explaining the relation between natural and spiritual knowledge.

An image of a plain, striving man concludes "Higher Laws," in a manner the co-author of *Walden* comes to expect. In this image, a negative movement of thought is recovered and transformed, and the severity of its discussion brought to a positive resolution on the next more subtle level. Here, in an actively ethical context, the identity of this plain striving everyman, "John Farmer," once more plumbs the profound psychological doubleness examined earlier in "Solitude." At the close of a day of hard work, having bathed, he sits at his doorstep, listening to the music of a flute, recollecting his thoughts—his own, of course—and the Spectator watches. The music comes "home to his ears out of a different sphere from that he worked in" and induces a reverie. "But how," Thoreau asks, "to come out of this condition and actually migrate thither?"

Just as "Solitude" led to a knowledge of our inner being (and to "Visitors" from the other world), "Higher Laws" leads to an analogous knowledge of the outer world (and to a complementary moral code necessary for life among "Brute Neighbors"). Here Thoreau is fishing for himself, as in "The Ponds," "communicating by a long flaxen line with mysterious nocturnal fishes" called ideas. His conclusion returns to the need not to be "the slave and prisoner of his own opinion of himself," so that the change that is communication can occur: "And all he could think of was to practise some new austerity, to let his mind descend into his body and redeem it, and treat himself with ever increasing respect." Higher laws are essentially the rules of self-respect.

These structural parallels extend to include the relationship between "Higher Laws" and the subsequent chapter, "Brute Neighbors," which follows on its own earthy plane, just as "Visitors" follows "Solitude." The movement of these larger parallels also passes through a zone of apparent opposition of morality to brutality. But we pass into a new gravitational field and hear a second dialogue between a Hermit and a Poet, who are as much facets of Thoreau's own personality as they are Thoreau and an actual companion. John Farmer's higher meditations on self-realization look forward to the Poet's meditations on hooking brutes with the truth. From one chapter to the next, both thinkers are at work on the same problem, though from different points of view. But likenesses such as these, which link the two last chapters of *Walden's* second phase, go far beyond their immediate connective function and enter into widening structural correspondences encircling the whole of the book.

The internal explorations conducted in *Walden's* first group of six chapters naturally lead to a study of *self*, one's own and those of others, and eventually of the transcendental Self, the Spectator. A complementary course is followed in the second group of six chapters. The inner thoughts give way to outer deeds, which become embodied thoughts; and animals replace people and become vehicles of vital ideas. Just as thoughts people the mind, animals carry thoughts into the world; and Thoreau ponders why animals "are all beasts of burden, in a sense, made to carry some portion of our thoughts," each transporting an idea from God to humanity. Both serial groups of chapters, however, are intimately modified by their contexts, spatially and mentally. In "Solitude" Thoreau's discussion of exactly *what* is "next to us" qualifies the identity of "Visitors" as spiritual, and in this way looks forward to the parallel qualification of our "Brute Neighbors" as physical.

The allegories of Thoreau's hounds, cats, loons, and especially his warring ants comprise rich and provocatively biographical fables, which are as much about people and society in general as are the more obvious lives of woodchoppers and village idiots. The three warring ants "united for life" "in deadly combat ... as if they had been men" hint at the human triangle of Ellen Sewall, John Thoreau, and Henry, who suggestively remarks, "The more you think of it, the less the difference." On many levels, then, these matched sets of chapters carry two progressively symmetrical lines of thought to parallel conclusions in different directions.

With the end of "Brute Neighbors" Thoreau concludes the second group of six chapters. This most positive phase of his book completes his survey of the two great divisions of human life—knowledge and experience. These complementary divisions in *Walden* mirror one another in their structure, movement, and meaning. The first, inner exploration, however, claims a natural priority, because it becomes the instrument of the second, outer exploration, by providing the self-knowledge necessary to examine the world. Both sections are clearly of equal literary merit. But taken together as tactical sequences, they exemplify Thoreau's communicative strategy on its largest scale. Overall, *Walden*'s first six chapters take a negative course in progressively sloughing off the ignorance of wrong-headed certainties, while the next six take a positive course in examining what the world looks like once these lower certainties have been replaced with an expanding knowledge of higher laws. *Walden*'s third section, as we will see, completes the philosophical leap with a trinitarian reconciliation of both views. The last six chapters answer a question Thoreau raises in "Economy": "Is it impossible to combine the hardiness of these savages with the intellectualness of the civilized man?" Is the world useful? Can spirit rise from the earth? Is it wise to break Pythagoras' rule and to taste beans?

8
BENT NAILS AND
THE BARBED GUMPHUS

Walden's first chapter is said to epitomize the whole book. The truth behind this commonplace is explained by the connections among Thoreau's method, his language, and his message. The same can be said, however, about the framing of any part of the book, because the implications of his earlier statements generate a progression of interlocking patterns. If we touch anything real, we touch all of reality. In quite the same way, if we read any part of *Walden* well, we have read all of it. Actually reading all of it is better, of course, and more enjoyable, because seeing the whole in the part requires "more skill in extracting or inserting the moral" and "will task the reader more than any exercise which the customs of the day esteem." Nonetheless, by reason of the architecture of parts and wholes, the threefold resonance within each mansion in the house called *Walden*—each chapter, paragraph, sentence, even each turn of phrase—can now be restated in so many words as the pivotal point.

The integrity of Thoreau's intellectual house is pinned on this principle. The one transcendental nail above holds the many boards below in place. Thoreau anticipates the arching shape and the operation of the three major phases of *Walden* by making earlier use, on a smaller scale, of the chief relationships among them. The inner-outer polarity of introspection and action, which he develops in his first six chapters, becomes the very fulcrum of the relationship between these and the second six chapters. Similarly, the idea of reintegration, developed throughout both of *Walden*'s first two phases, is elevated into the governing theme of the third, where reconciliation and synthesis become primary. In general, thematic images that are elevated and expanded into controlling motifs in any one of the book's major phases appear in minor roles prior to their period of prominence and do not entirely disappear after they have done their job. The task of combining, whether it be the hardiness and the intellectualness of our dual nature or heaven or nature herself, provides a good example of this structural rhythm. The coming together of things, as one expression of enlightenment, prior to the appearance of integration as the central metaphor in the third, serves as the closing theme of each of the first two phases.

The last of the first six chapters, "Visitors," measures Thoreau's friends, the woodchopper and the village idiot, who, not without humor, measure the animal and the intellectual within each one of us, against the ultimate yardstick of omniscience. In the woodchopper Therien integration has not taken place: "In him the animal man chiefly was developed.... But the intellectual and what is called spiritual man in him were slumbering as in an infant.... And a child is not made a man, but kept a child." The fifth and sixth chapters of the second grouping conclude with similar images. John the Farmer decides "to let his mind descend into his body and redeem it," and in so doing meets himself as the nearest of brute neighbors—an encounter anticipated early in "Economy" by the fact that "the bad neighborhood to be avoided is our own scurvy selves." But redeeming the lower self is as difficult as overtaking a loon, who has the "time and ability to visit the bottom of the pond in its deepest part."

In the conclusion of the first sequence, Thoreau's sketch of his woodchopper friend identifies integration with growth and maturation, in a way which clearly anticipates the extended discussion in "Higher Laws" of the role of hunting and fishing in the education of youngsters. Further, Thoreau identifies immaturity with slumber; and this allows him not only to link waking up from sleep with integration but also to connect the conditions of wakefulness and integration with the processes of youth, growth, and education, all as facets of the same spiritual experience. This picking up of earlier images and themes is another important part of Thoreau's communicative technique.

"Every child begins the world again, to some extent," Thoreau writes in "Economy." Later in "The Village" he writes "Every man has to learn the points of compass again as often as he awakes, whether from sleep or any abstraction," "for a man needs only to be turned round once with his eyes shut in this world to be lost." It was, we should recall, the "landscape of my *infant* [emphasis added] dreams" that Thoreau sought to clothe in expression through hoeing his beans, in a field which was "the *connecting* [emphasis added] link between wild and cultivated." From a necessary and wholesome balance between "animal health and vigor distinct from the spiritual," loving "the wild not less than the good," in "Higher Laws" Thoreau conflates maturation and integration. His goal for young people is to "*make* them hunters, though sportsmen only at first, if possible, mighty hunters at last, so that they shall not find game large enough for them in this or any vegetable wilderness,—hunters as well as fishers of men."

In "Brute Neighbors" this hunting game is further developed in the dialogue between the Poet and his Hermit friend. The Poet allegorizes: "Those village worms are quite too large; a shiner[1] may make a meal off one without finding

---

1. A small freshwater "trash" fish with soft rather muddy tasting flesh.

the skewer." The Hermit's barbed reply connects the rising and falling of Walden Pond to the fishing for men, presumably, in town: "Well, then, let's be off. Shall we to the Concord? There's good sport there if the water be not too high." In "Conclusion" Thoreau explicates this allegory of hunting and growing-up with a rhetorical question of his own: "How long, pray, would a man hunt giraffes if he could?" How long, in other words, will it take him to grow up and to realize "it would be nobler game to shoot one's self." Taming and integrating the lower self is the name of the game.

This punning answer goes a long way toward identifying the real, as opposed to the merely vegetable, wilderness, as nothing less than our unintegrated, because unregenerate state of being. But as this exchange between Poet and Hermit weaves hunting and maturing into a thematic analysis of personal integration, its structural resonances also recall an analogous internal dialogue in "Visitors," which carries the problem of integration onto the metaphysical level. Considering his brute neighbors, Thoreau wonders, "Why do precisely these objects which we behold make a world?" It is not by accident that in each case the problems of integration, of combining worlds and unifying selves, are handled according to the dominant imagery of the particular phase in which they are taken up. In the first and predominantly inward looking six chapters, this theme is couched in terms of the psychological make-up of the mind; in the next six outward looking chapters it is expressed in terms of the make-up of the world; and in the third and final set of six chapters it will be handled openly in terms of integration. Also worthy of our attention here is the fact that "Solitude" and "Higher Laws," which immediately precede the anchor chapters six and twelve, present integration as participation in nature. In "Solitude" we read "Shall I not have intelligence with the earth? Am I not partly leaves and vegetable mould myself? What is the pill which will keep us well, serene, contented?" And in "Higher Laws," "Fishermen, hunters, woodchoppers, and others, spending their lives in the fields and woods, [are] in a peculiar sense a part of Nature themselves."

The extent to which we are in fact *vegetable mould* receives its full—and critically overworked—answer in "Spring," where the warming earth anticipates the ultimate integration of spirit and matter in the question "What is man but a mass of thawing clay?" Out of this integration with nature, moreover, Thoreau distills an elaborate medicinal imagery, as one more way to discuss atonement and the cure of souls. In "Higher Laws," however, the internal perspective of "Solitude" gives way to a practical course of action reflected in another question, "Why do you stay here and live this mean moiling life, when a glorious existence is possible for you? … But how to come out of this condition and actually migrate thither?" "Spring" will later answer this question too, but foremost here is the way Thoreau uses analogous structural elements upon several levels of reference and toward several ends, all at the same time. His strategic questions not only connect the three larger phases of *Walden* and link chapters within them but they also enter into the *volatile truth* for which the entire book is the foundation and *residual statement.*

Not everyone, alas, is convinced that *Walden* is so well framed, and it is again no accident—it never is—that they object for reasons symbolized by a reportedly large but residual number of bent nails found about the foundation of Thoreau's cabin. Returning from *Walden* "with light baskets," having "baited their hooks with darkness," many a "professor in our colleges" exchange knowing looks and impugn Thoreau's ability to pound a nail straight. But picturing Thoreau as an inept intellectual who couldn't hit a nail on the head reveals a woeful ignorance of nails as well as a mean spirit. For Thoreau uses two kinds of nails, one for his cabin and another for his book. He built his cabin at Walden Pond using old-fashioned cut nails. These are made of low-grade iron; they have flat sides, rust irregularly, and bend easily. He framed his book using the *gumphus*, which is the fastener of choice for houses not built with hands. People familiar only with modern hardware miss the difference between the historical nail and the timeless *gumphus*, and, therefore, blame Thoreau with being all thumbs. (Construction projects at Emerson's house evoke similar sneers. If Thoreau bent nails, then, you know, he was a duffer like the rest of us.) Clearly, the sticking point is not cabins but transcendental carpentry. "But why," in Thoreau's words, "do I stay to mention these things?"

The difference between a nail and a *gumphus* needs to be driven home. The one comes from and returns to the earth, the other comes from the head and returns to heaven. In *Walden* "head is hands and feet," and thoughts are hammer and nails. Although Thoreau speaks like another carpenter in saying that "every nail driven should be as another rivet in the machine of the universe, you carrying on the work," we know how *Walden* was built from his remark that he did "not wish to be any more busy with my hands than necessary." A *gumphus* never bends or rusts, and holds like no nail ever can, because *above* pins *below* together by hooking back up to heaven. Bent nails are an emblem of the barbed *gumphus* used to fish for men and to frame castles in the air.

9
CENTRAL HEATING

So far, tracing parallels and following internal symmetries within and between *Walden*'s first two phases has necessarily postponed looking at the relationship the third bears to these. If the first paragraph of *Walden* epitomizes the whole book, then so also do its three major communicative divisions. Just as Thoreau brings each chapter to a positive conclusion, and each major phase to a complementary integration, he constructs the final six chapters, beginning with "House-Warming," so as to integrate all eighteen chapters into the unity of the whole of his book.

In *Walden* "the very globe continually transcends and translates itself, and becomes winged in its orbit." As the book moves to its conclusion, images of sailing and circling creatures fill the air, and the wings of Thoreau's house are connected with appropriate symbolism in "House-Warming." An actual house-warming is an indoor, social event which brings people inside. In this vein the first chapter of this third division is more social and, in particular, more encompassing than the earlier social chapters, "Visitors" and "Brute Neighbors," which anchor *Walden*'s first two groups of six chapters. "House-Warming" introduces the final six chapters, which bring the book full circle.

A house-warming is, moreover, a culminating event, which at last turns a newly built house into a home, changing a seasonal building into a year-round residence. A house-warming is also a kind of birth. And Thoreau reminds us of this when, in laying the foundation for his chimney, he records his allegorical surprise "to see ... how many pail-fuls of water it takes to christen a new hearth." The human body, of course, is the homological house and hearth where the vital heat must be maintained to give the soul a warm welcome. This chapter and its title accomplish as well as announce the completion of *Walden* as the body and house of Thoreau's thoughts. In this and the chapters that follow, as winter approaches, Thoreau finishes his house. In this masonic project, book, man, and nature move forward together toward completion. As he gathers "whiter and cleaner sand ... from the opposite shore of the pond," snow falls, winter assures that the pond is "skimmed over" with ice, and Thoreau plasters the walls of his house, and in so doing finishes the pages of his book.

By the equivalence of these converging activities we are once more reminded that in *Walden* the pattern is always *as above, so below*. The *whiter and cleaner sand ... from the opposite shore of the pond* with which Thoreau finishes the walls of his house is the objective correlative of the spiritual visitors with which he fills out his transcendental society. "I had withdrawn so far within the great ocean of solitude ... that ... only the finest sediment was deposited around me ... of unexplored and uncultivated continents on the other side." He homologizes, "I did not plaster till it was freezing weather.... The pond had in the meanwhile skimmed over.... I was pleased to see my work rising so square and solid by degrees, and reflected, that, if it proceeded slowly, it was calculated to endure a long time." The phrase *my work* includes *Walden*, of course, and the task of writing *Walden*, which was effectively completed toward the end of the life it cost him to write it.

His play upon the words *degrees* and *reflected*, deliberately extended in an identification of his house as his own "shell" and "crystallization," argues the same. As the world freezes over with the new "first ice" of a harder age, Thoreau, with curiously self-effacing yet unhumble allusions, displays his relentless curiosity as he allegorizes "Walden ice" into "two ices," "lower" and "upper," in anticipation of "Cambridge ice." Commenting on the air that is often trapped in the ice as it forms, with *A Week* and *Walden* not far in the background, he observes the "position my great bubbles occupied" in relation to the "many small bubbles" which "had burst out downward." Like the myriad lesser writers living their lives of "quiet desperation" and noisy failure, as biological and spiritual winter comes on, an "infinite number of minute bubbles," though "now frozen in likewise," "each, in its degree, demonstrating some life and affecting the world in some way," "had operated like a burning-glass on the ice beneath to melt and rot it." Yet, even the moral decay of those whose lives have *burst downward* provides a kind of human compost in which these very *bubbles*, as their own "former inhabitants," may someday burn upward and grow beans.

Thus is the task of plastering made to serve a homological purpose in Thoreau's spiritual allegory. In this instance, synthesis and maturation are combined with the image of his dwelling and its completion, as in "Higher Laws" these same themes were taken up with the figure of fishing. Even in "House-Warming," Thoreau is still digging for "fishworms." We should not be surprised, then, when Thoreau befriends "arrowy white pines, still in their *youth* [emphasis added]," and severally suitable for hunting, by chopping them down. He is more "the friend than the foe," for he has selected them for a higher role in his home, which is "a place of warmth, or comfort, first of physical warmth, then the warmth of the affections." The vital heat of "Economy" remains to the end the only truly economical way to heat any house.

Following the patterns established in "House-Warming," the final division completes the overall picture of *Walden.* Because these six chapters tie the whole book, as well as themselves, together, the net of implication exhibited by their lines of thought and knots of ideas is more complex and subtle and therefore more difficult to delineate. Even though speaking and meaning are conterminous activities, focusing upon communication as such competes with showing the very means by which it is achieved, while focusing upon the means has the converse effect of obscuring the message and communicative force of the whole work. As *Walden* leafs its way toward completion, the insight informing Thoreau's imagery and themes becomes more than mystical because it remains empirical. His images grow compound like the florets composing a sunflower. And the continuo of Thoreau's message resounds like the vernal music of the ice breaking up on Walden Pond, which made "a low and seemingly very distant sound, but singularly grand and impressive ... gradually swelling and increasing as if it would have a universal and memorable ending." A similar crescendo concludes Thoreau's book.

The homologous themes that flare up and illuminate this final section of *Walden* all originate in the *fire* lit in "House-Warming." Although at the outset Thoreau admits that "I never assisted the sun materially in his rising," it is with explicit homology that he makes the completion of his house parallel and assist the round of nature as well as the cycle of man and book. When, at the approach of winter, life retreats into matter, Thoreau retreats into the withdrawing room of his own chrysalis. "I withdrew yet farther into my shell, and endeavored to keep a bright fire both within my house and within my breast." Allegorically, his chimney and hearth, as the altar and winter residence of the vital heat, are the last parts of his house to be completed. To be sure, Thoreau works with secondhand bricks from the past and is struck by the many "violent blows" required to prepare them for new uses. But that is because he is writing sartorial archeology fit for blockheaded readers.

This connection between withdrawal and the "vital heat," of course, echoes throughout *Walden*—in "Economy," where vital heat and life are first purified, in "Where I Lived, and What I Lived For," where we learn to live in a "withdrawn … part of the universe," in "Solitude," where we learn to be really alone, and again in "Visitors," where we retreat to our withdrawing room. But carrying these anticipations even further, into a parable about the democracy of wood, Thoreau returns to the question of integrating mind and body.

> It is now many years that men have resorted to the forest for fuel and the materials of the arts: the New Englander and the New Hollander, the Parisian and the Celt, the farmer and Robin Hood, Goody Blake and Harry Gill; in most parts of the world the prince and the peasant, the scholar and the savage, equally require still a few sticks from the forest to warm them and cook their food. Neither could I do without them.

Thoreau's *neither could I* underscores the integration implied by this passage. Historical periods, nations, social classes, even the animal and intellectual within the individual are all linked by the universal need of *wood*. As certain sages say, the world is made of wood. Its necessary heat, further, not only links the two sides of being, but also joins being to nature, "for even the wildest animals love comfort and warmth as well as man, and they survive the winter only because they are so careful to secure them."

To say that wood fires the furnace which generates vital heat is but another way of declaring our unity with vegetable mould. But thus does Thoreau make fire, the immemorial sign of life, function as a universal instrument of preservation, integration, and that continuity called communication. The brilliance of his imagery becomes inescapable when we recall his Promethean pronouncement: "I desire to speak somewhere *without* bounds; like a man in a waking moment to men in their waking moments," for Prometheus was punished for bringing the fire of intelligence to humanity. The rising smoke from his chimney signifies that he is warm, alive, and therefore awake: "When the villagers were lighting their fires beyond the horizon, I too gave notice to the various wild inhabitants of Walden vale, by a smoky streamer from my chimney, that I was awake."

"House-Warming" ends with a picture of Thoreau beside his winter hearth, gazing into the flames. The light of his fire is "life imaging"—it rises from within, up through matter, lending it life and form, and then falls back into ashes, which denote there was a fire. Unsuspected "food for fire is still concealed in the bowels of the earth," because as *Walden* concludes "There is more day to dawn," and more lives to live. Returning from his winter walks, Thoreau would find his companion fire "still alive and glowing." The Spectator is watching. From this elegiac note of the passing of time and life, Thoreau moves logically to "Former Inhabitants; and Winter Visitors," and to a review of those flame-like flashes of life who have risen out of the Concord soil only to fall back into the earth. He has carefully prepared for this *ubi sunt* theme. He sets the stage for this age-old question, "Where are?" in *Walden*'s second (and first double) chapter, "Where I Lived, and What I Lived For." There he in fact lays the first brick of his hearth when he reminds us that "the future inhabitants of this region, wherever they may place their houses, may be sure that they have been anticipated."

Along the same line of recollection, in "Reading" he further remarks that he gazes "upon as fresh a glory" as any ancient philosopher; and earlier in "Economy" he chides the religious zealot who thinks his the only "second birth" and forgets that "Zoroaster, thousands of years ago, travelled the same road and had the same experience." His hoeing of beans disturbs the arrowheads of "an extinct nation." Now, beside his winter fire, Thoreau ponders the course of life through the world of matter: "The ghosts who from the dim past walked, and with us by the unequal light of the old wood fire talked." New-world wood should burn brighter, but the past is also part of the present; it too must be integrated with the other eternity in the full experience of *now.* "You can always see a face in the fire."

We can see how Thoreau's next and second double chapter, "Former Inhabitants; and Winter Visitors," opens with what appears to be two contrasting ideas: the past and the persistence of the past full of things and creatures outwardly crumbled, dead, and gone. But these are brought together when with Thoreau we search the faces staring at us from out of the fire. His statement that "for human society I was obliged to conjure up the former inhabitants of these woods" comments on his living neighbors as well as the remoteness of his cabin. Past and present are joined in a series of house-warming images.

Wood, in the form of a foundation of logs, still lies under the modern road, productive orchards spring from the stock of abandoned trees, new wheat sprouts from Egyptian mummies, and bugs crawl out of tables. And it is "here, by the very corner of my field" that the dramas of past life were lived out and are now relived with unblinking specificity— "east of my bean-field" and just "down the road, on the right hand, on Brister's Hill." Thoreau reinforces the vital

126

continuity and presence of past life with a vivid geographic reference: *all* this is still right here, and not so long ago and far away as we are wont to think and sometimes wish. Each timeless life is evoked and its course traced with stunning brevity. In each case, moreover, the life is depicted as an experiment of nature and one related to Thoreau. His life, his presence at Walden Pond, and his own house are presented as but the most recent of nature's creations. Phrases like "nearer yet to town," "farther down the hill," "farther in the woods than any of these," and "the last inhabitant of these woods before me," introduce the paragraphs in this chapter. Such spatial language, again, brings a landscape of elegiac vistas back to life as it leads us back to Thoreau, his book, and ourselves.

In addition to this elegiac mingling of biography, history, and geography, Thoreau interjects a philosophical *as-above* question, summarizing the problematic *so-below* careers of his characters as microcosmic villages within themselves. This time the music from "different spheres" which "did away with the street, the village, and the state" prompts him to rephrase John Farmer's question. He does not ask how to leave this "mean moiling life" "and actually migrate thither," but rather: "But this small village, germ of something more, why did it fail while Concord keeps its ground?" Why, in other words, did this group of people fail and like small bubbles in ice "burst out downward"?

In each portrait Thoreau generalizes and, like Chaucer, also seizes upon some telling detail, some piece of evidence to answer this question: a cellar hole obscured by the growth of new pines, a few scattered bricks reminiscent of bones, the remnant of an unkept orchard, a broken pipe on a cold hearth, and most, telling of all, a covered well. "What a sorrowful act," he exclaims with uncharacteristic sentiment, "must that be, —the covering up of wells! coincident with the opening of wells of tears." Yet these symbolic springs of life, around which "fate, free will, [and] fore-knowledge absolute, in some form and dialect or other were by turns discussed," are certain to be rediscovered and uncovered "some late day." To epitomize these truly moving narratives, Thoreau—did Whitman hear?—uses the lilac as another emblem for the continuity of life. "Still grows the vivacious lilac a generation after the door and lintel and the sill are gone, unfolding its sweet-scented flowers each spring, to be plucked by the musing traveller.... I marked its still tender, civil, cheerful, lilac colors."

Perhaps the most vivid of these miniature dramas, and the most central in terms of the vital heat and the continuity of life, is Thoreau's narration of the fire which consumed the "Codman Place." After flames had reduced the shabby family seat to ashes, an "heir of both its virtues and its vices" returned and gazed moaning upon the ruins, "as if there was some treasure, which he remembered, concealed between the stones, where there was absolutely nothing but a heap of bricks and ashes." Thoreau searches himself and Concord in the same way. In this up-dating of life's longing after life, of earth's longing after earth, he touches a number of truly immemorial themes that have shaped the English-speaking tradition. Nearly a thousand years ago, the *Beowulf* poet pondered:

> Gold for the gritty earth, where it still lasts,
> To men as useless—as ashes ever were.

And after him Middle English poets, more morbid than elegiac, complained, "Than hadde erthe of erthe erthe ynough." Thoreau is successful in "making the earth say beans instead of grass."

Thoreau passes on to the second part of this double chapter, "and Winter Visitors," in a way which reflects the similar movement between the divisions of his earlier double chapter. A fixed and external perspective is again internalized into a moving experience. Once more rising vapors become the symbol of life within. In "Where I Lived, and What I Lived For," "thin rising vapors" convinced Thoreau "that the richest vein is somewhere hereabouts," where *hereabouts* turns out to be books. Here in "Winter Visitors" he relates how during the great blizzard of 1717 a family was saved, because "the chimney's breath" found its way upward through the snowdrifts. Life works its way through matter. Even in his winter retreat, only the finest sediment reaches Thoreau through the snow. The finest natural men come to sit before Thoreau's fire, a hardy farmer "who donned a frock instead of a professor's gown," and a poet "who came farthest to my lodge," because and in spite of himself.

Smoke as the breath of a chimney is a universal image. We can easily find it in other cultures and seasons. The image occurs in a *haiku* of the eighteenth-century Japanese poet Gyodai.

Autumn mountains—	*Aki no yama*
Here and there	*tokorodokoro*
Smoke rising.	*kemuri tatsu*

But the way Thoreau brings this chapter to a close more readily recalls another earlier and better known Japanese poet, Matsuo Basho. Thoreau concludes with a picture of himself waiting for the ultimate "Visitor who never comes," while Basho depicts his own nostalgia for the inn built to receive but one guest. But like the poor heir of the burned Codman place, with Thoreau we all await the life which resides in the heat of the fire.

Since animal life is an expression of the larger life in nature, the next chapter, "Winter Animals," whose number include Thoreau of course, does not present a contradiction to its immediate predecessors. The owl in "Winter Visitors" prepares the way for his fellow creatures. He too is waiting, "looking out from the land of dreams." Even in the dead of winter nature is full of life and expectation. The owl is like Thoreau, who fled the village and sailed home through pines he could not see. The bird as well is "guided amid the pine boughs rather by a delicate sense of their neighborhood than by sight, feeling his twilight way, as it were, with his sensitive pinions." In this way, "he found a new perch, where he might in peace await the dawning of his day," and "there is more day to dawn." We feel that such a transcendental owl and Thoreau, as a Yankee Odysseus and student of Athena, have a great deal in common, above and beyond the way each moves through the forest, guided more by touch than by sight. Each in his own way is also waiting for his day. For Thoreau, every day "is an epitome of the year. The night is the winter, the morning and evening are the spring and fall, and the noon is the summer."

Thoreau too sails through the night, guided by his feet through the narrow gates of the pine forest, home through the blue gates, to claim his own. The memorial baying of racing hounds honors the faithful dog Argus. Their goings and comings disturb the winter woods, and like those of a poet, or of a loon, cannot be anticipated. Thoreau's hounds and other animals—his jays, squirrels, partridges, even the three symbolic creatures he lost long ago—all bespeak the life in nature, living on in spite of winter. Surely, Thoreau continued to pursue his "hound, a bay horse, and a turtle-dove," even into the winter of his own life. His partridge literally plunges into the snow; and when the bird disturbs the forest, snow "comes sifting down in the sunbeams like golden dust, for this brave bird is not to be scared by winter." Even the hare, "at first trembling with fear," abounds with energy. Yet all these winter animals are "of the very hue and substance of Nature, nearest allied to leaves and to the ground." Here Thoreau's question regarding the amount of "vegetable mould" in his own make-up finds an answer.

So far, in the first three chapters of *Walden*'s third phase, Thoreau has dealt with the integration of life, life brought indoors, but as real visiting "souls with their bodies." One after another, he has examined human life, past and present, nature's longer life, and animal life in nature, all of which are more than mutually inclusive neighbors. Next, in the fourth chapter, "The Pond in Winter," he turns to the deeper life of the earth itself. But in *Walden* space is "elastic," and opposite directions, if not mutually inclusive, are not mutually exclusive. Deeper may also mean higher, and other the same, so we should always expect both. Throughout his survey of life and its forms in this chapter, Thoreau again takes up and with new emphasis expands a number of familiar themes. Life is continuous, it is forever assuming new forms, but is never lost; life is also waiting and expectant, emitting subtle signs of its internal power; life is embodied by and embedded in matter, to the point where the two can be neither distinguished nor separated. In "The Pond in Winter" such themes as these are further developed toward what will be their full exfoliation in "Spring."

Earlier, in "The Ponds," Thoreau remarks that from the depths of Walden Pond, "a bright green weed is brought up on anchors even in midwinter." Now he makes still further use of this life under ice allegorized as matter. Seeking again to "drink at it," as from the shallow stream of time, with his axe he cuts a "a window under my feet, where, kneeling to drink," he reverently observes "the sandy bottom" in a new context, as a "bright sanded floor the same as in summer; there a perennial waveless serenity reigns." From this watery realm anglers draw "fabulous fishes," "like flowers and precious stones, as if they were pearls, the animalized *nuclei* or crystals of the Walden water." That these are caught, significantly, with "worms out of rotten logs," illustrates in still another way how hooking up to the power and value residing in what appears to be submerged and dead leads to more life.

In "The Pond in Winter" Thoreau returns to the pond as a focus and mirror of spiritual values, but this time in an even more intensely integrative idiom. Walden, the "lower heaven" where swimming is "a kind of flight or hovering," is now palpably central, since "Heaven is under our feet as well as over our heads." Yet, not entirely satisfied with the "pleasing mystery" of its depths, this time Thoreau is particularly "desirous to recover the long lost bottom of Walden Pond," or, in a word, to recover and firmly establish the "hard bottom and rocks in place" which support "the sandy bottom" of stars under the "thin current" of time. The *lost bottom* of things is their meaning.

His parable about sounding the pond and establishing its true depth by a careful examination of the shore confidently echoes his earlier allegorizing of the aesthetic value of Walden ice. Once more he asserts that the depths of the unknowable can become knowable through a right use of the surface of the known. It is possible, indeed, as the Middle Ages would put it, to read God's Book of Nature. It is the "immeasurable capacity for the marvelous" which we are unable to fathom in ourselves and, therefore, attribute to nature. Thoreau confirms Sir Philip Sidney's defense of poetry with the observation that "imagination, give it the least license, dives deeper and soars higher than Nature goes." As with *Walden*, reading any part of nature well is also to read it all. "If we knew all the laws of Nature, we should need only one fact, or the description of one actual phenomenon, to infer all the particular results at that point." A mountain has "an infinite number of profiles, though absolutely but one form." "What I have observed of the pond is no less true in ethics." Thus does Thoreau repeat the Mosaic parable of "Higher Laws." This time, he doesn't bring a string of fish back across the rainbow

bridge, rather like Beowulf, he finds the bottom, the meaning of the Walden Mere, returns with his trophy, and
applies it to life. Here, at Walden the world of opposites is
unified, and the duality of human nature is emblematically
resolved. Thoreau answers John Farmer's question with, "I
awoke to an answered question, to Nature and daylight....
I saw a double shadow of myself, one standing on the head
of the other, one on the ice, the other on the trees or hillside." This is the immemorial insight: Man is God upside
down.

"The Pond in Winter" closes appropriately—for "Spring"
is coming—with an episode of heroic ice-cutting. In a complex narrative ringing with Odyssean language and echoing with thematic images of economic cultivation, Thoreau
relates, and characterizes, another, wrong-headed harvest-
ing of Walden. Yet, because this wrong use of ice is merely
commercial, it is of no help in seeing the bottom. The
results are only superficial, even less than aesthetic, and
the deeper integration of cutting or seeing through any ice
is altogether missed. The perennial sources of life-giving
water remain untapped, and book-cutters are thereby
warned again. Thoreau has earlier observed that "the only
obvious employment" at Walden Pond was "ice-cutting, or
the like business." But now suddenly "there came a hundred men," who "meant to skim the land," or "to speak literally ... to get out the ice." And just as suddenly the ice-
cutters and their equipment are gone, and the ice is ironi-
cally left behind. Both ice and men are instantly translated
into former inhabitants of Walden vale, as they are swallowed up in the eternal abundance of nature. Walden
remains the same, "reflecting the clouds and the trees, and
sending up its evaporations in solitude, and no traces will
appear that a man has ever stood there."

Once more "rising vapors," as the symbol of the myriad
shapes and ascending continuity of life, communicate

Thoreau's meaning, specifically by concluding an episode and integrating its significance into the whole of *Walden*. Mingling "pure Walden water with the sacred water of the Ganges" echoes Thoreau's dwelling "nearer to those parts of the universe and to those eras of history which most attracted me." Co-authors who would seek the truth must break the ice at the "same well."

In the next chapter, "Spring," the house-warming motif finds its natural fulfillment, for spring is literally the warming of the world. The disgraced world of winter grows green in the renewing grass, which is at once a continuous "stream" as well as a purifying "flame." Thoreau's joining of "this perennial green stream" with the "spring fire" integrates the natural and divine energies manifesting in life and growth: the heat of the earth rises to join the heat of the sun. Several of Thoreau's thematic polarities—the arrowy white pines out of which he has framed his vision of life—come alive in a grand marriage of spirit and matter. The very earth is sensitive, "all alive with and covered with papillae." The flowing sandbanks testify to the same, as they respond to the heat of the heightening spring sun; the earth itself, internally impelled, flows into life-like forms. All things tend toward higher and higher expressions of themselves. The sand comes alive by flowing downhill and thus reminds us that to "burst out downward" is not always or ultimately bad, because that is what we must do to taste beans. Experience requires a living body. Now we gain a fuller understanding of how "the very globe continually transcends and translates itself, and becomes winged in its orbit." Misty, steaming fields "of russet and white smoking with incense" epitomize other rising vapors and reveal a universal elevation of life in which "there is nothing inorganic." All life issues its sacrificial prayer: "Go thou my incense upward from this hearth, and ask the gods to pardon this clear flame."

If we remember this prayer and allow that everything is *all alive*, then Thoreau has accomplished his goal and joined the two worlds. An unthinking belief that the apparent separateness of the natural and the ideal is real and permanent is precisely what defines the subtle mental rigidity that makes any human being "but the slave and prisoner of his own opinion of himself," and the world into a house of quiet desperation for too many of us.

As "Spring" progresses, Thoreau weaves his themes into a shimmering unity. Waking, for example, is brought to fullness in: "I am on the alert for the first signs of spring." These signs especially require that kind of strenuous reading described in *Walden*'s first six chapters, for spring speaks that "language which all things and events speak without metaphor, which alone is copious and standard." With a grand rhetorical question Thoreau reminds us that nobody can read the best books, let alone the book of nature, without being perpetually and truly awake: "What Champollion will decipher this hieroglyphic for us, that we may turn over a new leaf at last? ... What at such times are histories, chronologies, traditions, and all written revelations?"

Thoreau's waiting and watching for the "Visitor who never comes" captures the moment, at least, when His approaching footstep stamps spring upon the world, "seemingly instantaneous at last." "Suddenly," he reports, "an influx of light filled my house." And light communicates. All nature is affected by this double revelation. Even the returning geese are guided by Thoreau's achievement: "They suddenly spied my light, and with hushed clamor wheeled and settled in the pond." His human fellows, too, influenced by this communication of his enlightenment, exhibit a "holiness groping for expression." Thoreau finds new words for the immemorial spiritual truth that secret yet irresistible spiritual influences guide all creation toward higher states. "The symbol of an ancient man's thought becomes a modern man's speech." One well-organized institution will organize a country. Rulers have but to love virtue to inspire peace and order. And "when one man has reduced a fact of the imagination to be a fact to his understanding, I foresee that all men will at length establish their lives on that basis."

Other themes, besides these which deal more or less directly with communication, are taken up in "Spring" and worked toward a general summation in "Conclusion," which in its thematic complexity exhibits many a striking, complementary resemblance to "Economy." The question of loneliness is again engaged and answered: the ever-present marsh hawk is not lonely in its "ethereal flight"; rather it makes the earth lonely. The cure for our ills is another taste of "God's drop," the ultimate "tonic of wildness." A restatement of life's unsuspected abundance and secret meaning provides an introduction to the direct communicative concerns of "Conclusion."

> At the same time that we are earnest to explore and learn all things, we require that all things be mysterious and unexplorable, that land and sea be infinitely wild, unsurveyed and unfathomed by us because unfathomable. We can never have enough of nature. We must be refreshed by the sight of inexhaustible vigor, vast and titanic features, the sea-coast with its wrecks, the wilderness with its living and its decaying trees, the thundercloud, and the rain which lasts three weeks and produces freshets.

Each detail in Thoreau's inventory specifically recalls an earlier passage from his book. The *sea-coast with its wrecks*, for example, was exactly what Thoreau sought along the "headlands" of his own being, and what he found at Flint's Pond, "our greatest lake and inland sea," when "one day, as

I crept along its sedgy shore, the fresh spray blowing in my face, I came upon the mouldering wreck of a boat.... It was as impressive a wreck as one could imagine on the sea-shore, and had as good a moral." Similarly, echoing the conclusion of "Economy," where he refutes the philan-thropic objections to his way of life, Thoreau concludes "Spring" with an answer for those who will not accept a real nature in which "tender organizations can be so serenely squashed out of existence like pulp": "The impression made on a wise man is that of universal innocence.... Com-passion is a very untenable ground."

Thoreau is not being cruel—certainly not a Pollyanna transcendentalist—but only reminding us that reading and understanding life are not sentimental pastimes. "Spring" leads on to the heroic warmth of summer, "as one rambles into higher and higher grass." It is not merely taller grass that we should seek, but grass growing in higher fields. With the integration of the inner world of consciousness and the outer world of nature, Thoreau has completed his "house-warming." And in "Conclusion," summer warmth produces the final and permanent harvest of *Walden* beans.

10
PLASTERED
WITH PATIENCE

The actual impact of any work must grow out of its immediately accessible features. Whatever recondite excellencies retrospection may show a work to possess come second. Nonetheless, as powerfully obvious as the connection between "Spring" and "Conclusion" is, the way these two chapters fit together is not easily explained. To show further how form and meaning in *Walden* combine to connect "Conclusion," and the other five of the last six chapters, to the whole of the book is also a challenge. Even by the easy standards of "little reading," so many obvious excellences from every chapter deserve attention, that many hard illustrative choices must be made.

Thoreau's fire imagery comes immediately to mind. Vital and copious enough for Shakespeare, the image of fire signifies living thought, life in matter, past life, life in nature, and the apotheosis of all of these in the great spring of the world's present moment. Fire transmutes this entire natural world into the altar and fuel for the grand sacrifice: both the human mind and nature are consumed and rise into an ethereal existence, all ignited and enlightened by the "tinder of a mortal brain."

Going back for a moment, however, and taking a closer look, we can see that the connection between "Spring" and "Conclusion" is multifaceted and far-reaching. It proves, first, to be a special case of the encompassing relationship "Economy" and "Conclusion" bear to their respective groups of chapters and to *Walden* as a whole. The book's three major groups of chapters follow one another according to the rationale of Thoreau's effort to communicate new ideas. Modern men and women, in particular, trapped in the empirical case they suppose, have first to unlearn, to learn, by waking into an awareness of that consistent subjectivity called objectivity. Although catching on to the drift of Thoreau's thought is easy enough, no scholar-like thought can do justice to the working subtleties of the intricate communicative envelope his three terminal chapters together make up. The connections among "Spring" and "Conclusion" and the whole of *Walden* require a second, retrospective look. The elegant clarity of their arrangement saves even the most detailed analysis from obscurity.

Thoreau appears to make a clean break, for example, between the later chapters "Spring" and "Conclusion," while, on the other hand, to move without a break between the two introductory chapters, "Economy" and "Where I Lived, and What I Lived For." But the apparent want of symmetry this difference might suggest is resolved by *Walden*'s functional structure. In fact, there is a greater distance between "Economy" and its sequel, and a greater proximity between "Spring" and "Conclusion," than at first appears. "Economy" is recognized as notoriously preparatory, aimed as it is toward readying us for our own *Walden* co-adventure. But so in its own way is "Conclusion," which readies us for brighter days of even greater adventures anticipated by a rising sun which, as Thoreau reminds us, "is *but* [emphasis added] a morning star." For he refers to his "present" Walden adventure as "my next experiment of this kind" and later explains, "I left the woods for as good a reason as I went there. Perhaps it seemed to me that I had several more lives to live, and could not spare any more time for that one." No level of achievement in *Walden* is ever final. Actually, much of "Economy" describes Thoreau's preparation before he went to live at the pond and, therefore, precedes the Walden experiment as much as the experiences anticipated in "Conclusion" follow it. Thoreau's remarks in "Economy" and "Baker Farm" —"In short, I went on thus for a long time," "For more than five years," and "I thought of living there before I went to Walden"—show how gradual was his getting ready for his sudden move.

Reflecting this gradual haste, Thoreau does not engage his subject proper, his life in the woods, until his second chapter. The complemental verses closing "Economy" do not so much advance his preparation as they retrospectively mark the negative side of getting ready to be an azad, or free man, before this freedom is put to use. Yet "Economy" seems to move smoothly into "Where I Lived, and What I Lived For," because the discussion of place and purpose follows logically, and Thoreau, as it were, appears to repeat himself. The "spring of springs" and "a higher and more ethereal life" are first mentioned in "Economy" long before "Spring" arrives. Thoreau's habit is to look again and more subtly at what he has looked at before, so that the effects of this appositive motion create a sense of connection.

The more obvious break between "Spring" and "Conclusion" responds to a complementary analysis. Conversely, though greater, the break is not as great as it seems. For although Thoreau is careful to maintain the communicative immediacy of *me* and *you*, and begins *Walden*'s several sections with conversational phrases, occasionally this first to second person stance is transcended by the presence of the Spectator, "that is no more I than it is you." When this Spectator arrives, the descriptive distance of the past slips into an experience of the present. "At a certain season of our life" melts into "*this* [emphasis added] is a delicious evening," and we wonder just where we and Thoreau are. The full turn from "Visitors" to "The Bean-Field," perhaps, represents the most marked instance of this conversational re-grounding of narrative focus. Here, with "MEANWHILE my beans," we are brought from the heights of subjective experience "within the great ocean of solitude," where we can hardly be said to occupy our own body, to "burst[ing] out downward" into the solid daylight business of following the rest of the story.

In this connection, "Conclusion" accomplishes an even greater return, not just to the forward movement of the story, since what follows lies in any case beyond *Walden*, but to the original conversational framework with which *Walden* begins. We hear Thoreau's "first person" voice again saying "Moreover, I, on my side" and trying to "say something" to "you who read these pages." And since we have been "passengers who have a season ticket and see it often," we listen to the voice of *Walden* with wiser ears in this only world of waking experience. Still more, turning our attention back to "Economy," we can see that Thoreau's first chapter is preparatory in a twofold way, in which "Conclusion" is not abruptly final. Thoreau's move to the pond was mentally, even physically gradual, but when the time came, he followed his own advice to other poets to go "up [to the] garret at once." He left society "determined to go into business at once, and not wait." Like his namesake and alter ego, the "artist of Kouroo,"[1] "he proceeded instantly to the forest for wood," where aeons pass like minutes.

Because eternity is not just the forever of endless time, but something else outside of time, the proportions of Thoreau's bulletin from immortality reflect this same paradoxical equilibrium. *Walden* too begins gradually, but happens suddenly; ends abruptly, but continues. *Walden* is

---

1. Modern spelling: *Kuru*; see the *Bhagavad-Gîta*.

as "seemingly instantaneous," as transitory, yet as eternal, as the coming of Spring in spring. Our preparation, if its effects are to last, cannot be sudden; but our realization of its lesson necessarily must be. Like Thoreau, his co-authors must work slowly, building to last, up until the instant when the final nail is driven home. If "Olympus is but the outside of the earth everywhere," then forever is the "meeting of two eternities" now. "But all these times and places and occasions are now and here. God himself culminates in the present moment, and will never be more divine in the lapse of all the ages." Conclusions are beginnings.

"Conclusion," in its powerful recapitulation of images and ideas first introduced in "Economy" and sustained throughout, becomes *Walden*'s most positive and sudden chapter. The quiet groundswell of implication rising throughout the book breaks into a roar of explicit expression. Waves of meaning crash in upon us and carry us to the other shore. Without drowning in nice distinctions, however, or getting lost in the undertow of the obvious, we can appreciate the liquid and ample balance between *Walden*'s terminal chapters. Pondering complementary distinctions, we can come to understand the metaphysical reasons why the break preceding "Conclusion" seems greater and that following "Economy" seems smaller, and why the difference is important. There is an organic appropriateness attaching to the rhythms of *Walden*'s form, which is inseparable from its meaning. A body of a living soul is conceived at once, gestates slowly, is born at once, ages slowly, and dies at once, but only to continue elsewhere in another form. *Walden* presents just such a counterpoint of moment and duration, of visible and invisible change. The book resacralizes a life that seems to be nothing, but can change everything; it embraces a death that seems to be everything, but changes nothing. But why, like Thoreau, do we stay to mention these things?

Overlong explanations of wholeness may self-destruct, even though they pierce through to the powerful patterns "behind the plastering." The double helix of Thoreau's thought commands its own interest. The caducean motion of his tale never falls off, but quickens the very body of his book. And only a wag would coddle us with art or impugn our judgment by pretending that anything short of full understanding will do. An insight into the workings of Thoreau's mind sheds light on the secrets threading through his sentences, the golden braid binding his chapters, and the huge cables holding up the three larger groups of chapters, which comprise his book. The cumulative complexity of the third, integrative group is a necessary outcome of the progressive refinement and interweaving of these connections.

The measure of this concentric intricacy is the degree to which *Walden* becomes a book about a book. *Walden* merges ontology and epistemology into universalized autobiography. The chapters following "Brute Neighbors," which closes the book's second, natural phase, illustrate this involution. "House-Warming" comes next, and the final five chapters echo, recapitulate, and develop all that has gone before. At the same time they also command an appropriate local complexity, as they carry Thoreau's themes to final expression. The resultant merging of form, matter, and argument, early hinted in "Economy," is here realized. This rare unity becomes increasingly evident as *Walden* progresses. It receives early statement in "Reading" and "Sounds," and central demonstration in "The Ponds." But in "Conclusion" reflexive comments about *Walden* and its author reach an intensity that lays indirection aside, but saves subtlety. Thoreau's thoughts are no longer concealed behind the plastering, but emerge into open if double-edged self-compliment. An outline of *Walden*'s structure must conclude with a glance at this centripetal movement.

In "Spring" Thoreau arrives at a direct statement of what he has all along implied, for "the day is an epitome of the year." Each paragraph of "Conclusion" exemplifies the principle of *as above, so below*, to make this chapter into the grand epitome of *Walden* itself. If, for example, we have missed the allegorical import of "Still we live meanly, like ants," when we were reading in "Where I Lived, and What I Lived For," or the significance of the prolonged ant battle in "Brute Neighbors," surely we cannot escape the ghost of Jonathan Edwards[2] in the Calvinist resonance of Thoreau's insect imagery:

> As I stand over the insect crawling amid the pine nee-
> dles on the forest floor, and endeavoring to conceal it-
> self from my sight, and ask myself why it will cherish
> those humble thoughts, and hide its head from me
> who might, perhaps, be its benefactor, and impart to its
> race some cheering information, I am reminded of the
> greater Benefactor and Intelligence that stands over
> me the human insect.

Thoreau, of course, puts a potentially happy and unpuritanical face on the human predicament; but nonetheless, in this cosmogonal comparison the shift from implication to direct statement becomes clear.

The literal restatement of many other thematic metaphors can be used to show how "Conclusion" epitomizes the whole of *Walden*. The idea of desperation, which runs throughout the book—from the famous quiet desperation in his first chapter, "Economy," to "desperate haste to succeed and in such desperate enterprises" in his last, is

---

2. An eighteenth-century American preacher and educator notorious for a sermon entitled, "Sinners in the Hands of an Angry God," in which humanity is likened to a loathsome insect held at arm's reach by God over the pit of hell.

another obvious example. The image of the "paths that the mind travels," some form of which runs from chapter to chapter, is still another, among many more. Even here, however, when Thoreau's allegorical insects begin openly to bite and sting us with morality, the pain points to higher pleasures. These purposeful patterns and comments are to be found in those passages that speak with increasing directness to the communicative effectiveness of *Walden* as a book, and they include, often in openly epistemological language, a running commentary upon the nature and effectiveness of his own attempt to communicate through words. Any illustrative sequence chosen from among them confirms the marriage of form and idea which mark the book's communicative strategies.

Here, as indeed everywhere, in writing about *Walden* co-authors are faced with hard choices. Focussing upon one feature mutes or displaces another, so that foregrounding Thoreau's explicit commentary unavoidably neglects his implicit evaluations to the same effect. In "The Bean-Field," for example, Thoreau actually discusses the writing of *Walden* in terms of growing beans. Although he wanted only to taste rather than to subsist on beans, he congratulates himself that "I hoed them unusually well as far as I went, and was paid for it in the end." Hoeing beans includes digesting the fruit of his labors and recording them in *Walden*, which came out well, for this New England artist of Kouroo. Each "fine leaf" produced by a day's hoeing or writing became a "connecting link between wild and culti-vated fields" of author and reader. *Walden* was published, but the author paid the price of breaking Pythagoras' rule. Nonetheless, both his beans and his pages will "have results which are not harvested by me" when people read *Walden*. In "The Ponds" Thoreau makes another complimentary reference to his book, but this time he does so through the image of an older fisherman who is also Thoreau himself, or his best part. To similar effect Thoreau says, "I was equally pleased when he sat in my doorway to arrange his lines." Here again the lines arranged include the written lines of *Walden*. But from the beginning, in "Economy," we find Thoreau discussing the philosophical foundation of his book and its readership in language "without metaphor, which alone is copious and standard."

He begins with an epistemological outline of the mechanics of communicating and learning he intends to use. But the formula for acquiring new knowledge is also the algorithm for writing a book which communicates with others as well as oneself. A frank acknowledgment of the difficulties of communicating and a daunting appeal to co-authors run through "Economy."

> How can he remember well his ignorance—which his growth requires—who has so often to use his knowledge? ... One may almost doubt if the wisest man has learned anything of absolute value by living.... The whole ground of human life seems to have been gone over by their predecessors.... We might try our lives by a thousand simple tests.... If I had remembered this, it would have prevented some mistakes.... I sometimes despair of getting anything quite simple and honest done in this world by the help of men.

These animadversions have been met in other contexts, where their immediate function often obscures their larger communicative significance. But when they are juxtaposed, they reveal Thoreau's sustained efforts to communicate to his readers.

In "Where I Lived, and What I Lived For" Thoreau's interpretation of his Walden experience becomes somewhat more confident, but remains guarded in its expectations. He does make it clear, however, that the hills to be mined are books, in particular his book, which will be "somewhere hereabouts," because the reader will have it in hand. In this light his remark that "I think that the richest vein is somewhere hereabouts" assumes a bemusing self-reference.

> I know of no more encouraging fact than the unquestionable ability of man to elevate his life by a conscious endeavor.... I went to the woods because I wished to live deliberately.... I wanted to live deep and suck out all the marrow of life ... and, if it proved to be mean, why then to get the whole and genuine meanness of it, and publish its meanness to the world.

His direct commentary continues in "Reading," in an open challenge to the reader to understand that *Walden* is *not* another ordinary book, but scripture like that other good book. On the contrary, his book, he tells us, is more than mere rhetoric, as profound as the stars are high, and based upon immemorial ideas. These qualities require a matching depth in the reader. And, if *Walden* is read well—that is, as "deliberately and reservedly" as it was written—it will yield esoteric truths.

> However much we may admire the orator's occasional bursts of eloquence, the noblest written words are commonly as far behind or above the fleeting spoken language as the firmament with its stars is behind the clouds. *There* are the stars, and they who can may read them.... The symbol of an ancient man's thought becomes a modern man's speech.... The works of the great poets have never yet been read by mankind, for only great poets can read them.... The book exists for us, perchance, which will explain our miracles and reveal new ones. The at present unutterable things we may find somewhere uttered.

Somewhere points to *Walden,* the book which is *somewhere hereabouts.* It is not really "a ground for complaint if a man's writings admit of more than one interpretation."

In "Sounds" Thoreau the practical teacher and experienced author of the unsuccessful *A Week on the Concord and Merrimack Rivers* ruminates prophetically upon the prospects of a book like *Walden.* Effective communication requires change, it also requires an audience. But as Thoreau says later in "Conclusion," he is not overly optimistic that he will ever be able to speak "like a man in a waking moment, to men in their waking moments." In the moralizing context of "Sounds," however, he confesses that "practically speaking, when I have learned a man's real disposition, I have no hopes of changing it for the better or worse in this state of existence." In "Higher Laws" Thoreau turns to the paradoxical power of language itself. He is not sure that words as words, that is, someone else's words, can effect any necessary changes, which can come only from within.

> Perhaps the facts most astounding and most real are never communicated by man to man.... I hesitate to say these things, but it is not because of the subject, —I care not how obscene my *words* are, —but because I cannot speak of them without betraying my impurity.... We are all sculptors and painters, and our material is our own flesh and blood and bones.

In "House-Warming" Thoreau returns to the subject of language and its literal and figurative senses.

> It would seem as if the very language of our parlors would lose all its nerve and degenerate into *palaver* wholly, our lives pass at such remoteness from its symbols, and its metaphors and tropes are necessarily so far fetched, through slides and dumb-waiters, as it were; in

other words, the parlor is so far from the kitchen and workshop. The dinner even is only the parable of a dinner, commonly. As if only the savage dwelt near enough to Nature and Truth to borrow a trope from them. How can the scholar, who dwells away in the North West Territory or the Isle of Man, tell what is parliamentary in the kitchen?

The knowledge that Thoreau regarded himself as his own "parable-maker," sharpens his alimentary play upon *palaver*, which derives from "parable," and brings the metaphysics of his humor to bear upon *Walden* as an act of communication.

Finally, in "Conclusion" Thoreau, not one to mince his words, says *in other words* that *Walden* may be difficult, but that he will still find readers, because "it is a ridiculous demand which England and America make, that you shall speak so that they can understand you. Neither men nor toadstools grow so. As if that were important, and there were not enough to understand you without them." It is not surprising that the Longfellows, the Lowells, and many a modern professor-critic hate Thoreau with a passion, since no one likes to be lumped together and labelled: "safety in stupidity alone."

Thoreau goes on to express his belief that if spiritual knowledge is private, we can at least talk to ourselves, even if language may not be the primary *parlor* nor words the instruments of more than *palaver*. He summarizes with "I left the woods for as good a reason as I went there.... I learned this, at least, by my experiment: that if one advances confidently in the direction of his dreams, and endeavors to live the life which he has imagined, he will meet with a success unexpected in common hours." Thoreau, at least has learned something, and he is confident his reader also can. This self-referential discussion of his own book, however, has the collective effect of inviting the reader into Thoreau's confidence as co-author. This role compounds the entire process of communicating through words.

In this same vein Thoreau re-examines our actual predicament in relation to the status of words as boundary phenomena between us and higher truths. Words or at least the bottom half of them belong to the world of forms. Words alone cannot, therefore, convey the higher forms which reach beyond the three earthly dimensions.[3] Although Thoreau graduated from Harvard, he is not saying, however, that words create meaning through some kind of agnostic groping. When Thoreau says that he wishes he could speak somewhere *without* bounds, he is suggesting that his words have more than one interpretation. But he is also suggesting a purposefulness by which these interpretations arrange themselves according to lower and higher laws. First, socially, he means that he wishes he could speak and not be limited by unimaginative readers. Second, logically, he means that he wishes he could speak without leaping to false conclusions. Third, metaphysically, he means that he wishes he could speak outside ordinary meaning.

> For the most part, we are not where we are, but in a false position. Through an infirmity of our natures, we suppose a case, and put ourselves into it, and hence are in two cases at the same time, and it is doubly difficult to get out.... We know not where we are.... I fear chiefly lest my expression may not be *extra-vagant* enough.... I desire to speak somewhere *without* bounds.... The volatile truth of our words should continually betray the inadequacy of the residual statement. Their truth is

---

3. The Sanskrit terms *rūpa*, "form," and *arūpa*, "other than form," are useful here.

instantly *translated*: its literal monument alone remains. The words which express our faith and piety are not definite; yet they are significant and fragrant like frankincense to superior natures.

Thoreau's relativist and aesthetic critics, it is important to repeat, stumble here on his statements that words have "different senses" and "admit of more than one interpretation." Their own epistemology, *doubly difficult to get out of,* causes them to presume that Thoreau views language the same way they do. But he is no agnostic pluralist, so that his language is never arbitrary, opaque, or merely conventional, because his knowledge includes but also exceeds the bounds of sense perception. Thoreau is telling us nothing less than that he has all the time been writing allegory and speaking in cipher. Thoreau is never more biblical than when he touches upon the subject of ears and hearing. "The morning wind forever blows, the poem of creation is uninterrupted; but few are the ears that hear it."

But the image that makes the frankest, most unembarrassedly powerful self-referential, and most pertinent case for communication as essential change, and for Thoreau's effort to effect such change, is the "artist in the city of Kouroo." This symbolic figure, through utter devotion to the task, carves a walking stick into the universe. The artist is none other than Thoreau, again, or his real co-author-reader, and his walking stick is *Walden* itself. Point for point this allegory recapitulates the structure of the book. Chips of wood play an important role throughout *Walden*. They flew when Thoreau first struck out his house; he and his poet friend leave a pile of them after conversing; the death struggle of three ants takes place on one; and now a pile of chips becomes the universe itself! Having "left the woods for as good a reason as I went," Thoreau tells us that there are greater morning tasks waiting to be done. Proceeding "instantly to the forest for wood," he has worked with great diligence. Having finished his task, he asks, "but why do I stay to mention these things?" Every "artist in the city of Kouroo" wants to communicate metaphysics to materialists, and Thoreau is astonished at his own achievement.

When the finishing stroke was put to his work, it suddenly expanded before the eyes of the astonished artist into the fairest of all the creations of Brahma. He had made a new system in making a staff, a world with full and fair proportions; in which, though the old cities and dynasties had passed away, fairer and more glorious ones had taken their places. And now he saw by the heap of shavings still fresh at his feet, that, for him and his work, the former lapse of time had been an illusion, and that no more time had elapsed than is required for a single scintillation from the brain of Brahma to fall on and inflame the tinder of a mortal brain. The material was pure, and his art was pure; how could the result be other than wonderful?

The declarations of this passage, read as "deliberately and reservedly as they were written," comprise a biography of the author, an analysis of his book, a history of the universe, and a measure not only of Thoreau's co-authors but Thoreau himself as Co-author. And like the laths behind the plaster, these all hold together.

11
UNITY OF
EQUIVALENCE

What holds *Walden* together has been traced in Thoreau's desire to communicate "some cheering information." As the book progresses, this desire shapes *Walden* more and more intimately. First and foremost, *Walden* is a highly unified act of communication. But there are many ways to unify a book. To show how *Walden* works, we have looked at the representative images, thematic repetitions, and structural patterns that communicate the metaphysical connections in and among *Walden*'s several chapters and chapter groupings. As Thoreau himself says with precarious frequency, language itself is something of a cemetery by the sea for the "finest sediment" of meaning, the "literal monument" and "residual statement" of the book's "volatile truth." Still, even though *Walden* works, and works well, the book is much more than a literary machine.

At the same time, if *Walden* is not a machine, the impact the book has upon people argues, on the other hand, for something deeper than literary unity. The beauties of Thoreau's book are more than aesthetic, and its priorities more than pluralistic. Thoreau's high view of art would have it so, and his dialectic requires it. Not least of the contradictions surrounding *Walden* is that the author of its undeniably great art, having outgrown the so-called fine arts, has become *anti*-aesthetic or, more precisely, *post*-aesthetic.

For, as Thoreau says, "the value of a man is not in his skin, that we should *touch* him [emphasis added]." Art involves the use as well as the enjoyment of surfaces. Thoreau's achievement lies in his forcing language to its upper limits and there, by subtle paralinguistic inversion, making words say much more than they ordinarily do. At the same time, he accomplishes this feat by changing his readers into co-authors who will change their words. For these reasons the description of the upper "volatile" senses of Thoreau's words fly off into transcendental *experience.*

We must, therefore, begin and end by asking into what precisely is verbal truth translated? The fact that *Walden* overflows with clues does not, necessarily, make an answer any easier. One set of clues is found in Thoreau's frequent and specific insistence upon the distinction between literal and figurative statements. For example, he concludes his mock-epic ice-cutting episode involving "a hundred man of Hyperborean extraction," with "to speak literally, a hundred Irishmen." "It is true," he earlier insists, "I never assisted the sun materially." Applied to "what remains to remind us," that is, to the verbal monument of *Walden,* these and other statements like them direct the search for meaning beyond the forms of language.

Thoreau also insists upon the "difference between affections and the intellect." Emotional excitement alone is no more understanding than "stupidity alone." Head, heart, and hand must all work together, so that experience is known, felt, and grasped. Thoreau, as the writer, is interested in all in any age who can *understand* him. As far as books go:

> It is not enough even to be able to speak the language of that nation by which they are written, for there is a memorable interval between the spoken and the written language, the language heard and the language read. The one is commonly transitory, a sound, a tongue, a

dialect merely, almost brutish, and we learn it unconsciously, like the brutes, from our mothers. The other is
the maturity and experience of that; if that is our
mother tongue, this is our father tongue, a reserved
and select expression, too significant to be heard by the
ear, which we must be born again in order to speak.

Regardless of what language may be like among the *brutes*,
Thoreau identifies *his* language in a very traditional way.
There is indeed a wisdom surpassing understanding, but
words restored to their unfallen best can rise up into it,
because mind and world are both expressions of the Logos,
and the polarity between them is so constructed as to allow
final participation. This is why words can be remarkable
lenses. They are the mental equivalent of the ice on
Walden Pond, which Thoreau allegorizes into the reality of
surfaces. The visible world in its intermediate linking position enables us to see the bottom of things and, since
heaven lies in all directions, the top as well.

Thoreau's communicative use of "ice" shows that he
regards it as "an interesting subject for contemplation," as
indeed the uses of the world and language are. Consequently, as he brings *Walden* to a close, we find him con-
structing another parable about ice, this time in order to
explain why people complain "if a man's writings admit of
more than one interpretation," as his surely do, and why
people have not taken him at his word about his own
words. Unlike Walden ice, he tells us, is "Cambridge ice,
which is white, but tastes of weeds," because it is harvested
from a shallow pond clogged with communicable scholar-
like thoughts. If people won't spend enough life to buy
"Walden ice," they will get only what they pay for and must
be satisfied with damaging their poverty without being rich.
But we have only to recall a few of Thoreau's pivotal metaphors to see the "azure ether" gleaming through "the mists

which envelop the earth." This is how his language works. His images—of clothing, business, cultivation, fishing and hunting, architecture and building, rivers, ponds, woods, rainbows, and even the stars—all command a useful inter-relatedness, and to such a degree that they merge into identities with a difference. Like smoke and rising vapors, things translate into ideas. Particular images converge, rise and coalesce into themes, themes expand into arguments, and arguments shape themselves into the higher architec-ture of his castles in the air. Thoreau has asked in many ways "why do precisely these objects which we behold make a world?" They do because they and the world itself are really expressions of the one Idea, and as such they become unique "beasts of burden." As Thoreau says, every word inhabiting his woods is "in a sense," that is, through our senses and the ranks of meaning accessible through them, "made to carry some portion of our thoughts."

The figure of the arch is another such linguistic beast. To understand why this is so, we must participate in Thoreau's search for readers who could *understand* him. Thoreau builds many arches throughout *Walden* and so places them, that they provide the intellectual vaulting which supports his book's highest levels of meaning.

> Should not every apartment in which man dwells be lofty enough to create some obscurity overhead, where flicker-ing shadows may play at evening about the rafters?

At first he presents arches as means of surmounting igno-rance. "If necessary," he advises, "omit one bridge over the river, go round a little there, and throw one arch at least over the darker gulf of ignorance which surrounds us." Then he selects the "lower heaven all the more important" of Walden Pond as the proximate pedestal, so to speak, on this side of truth. Walden, pond and book, is suitable for this purpose, because "It is a good port and a good foundation," since there we can come to a hard bottom and rocks in place and build "castles in the air for which earth offered no worthy foundation." Even if we sink into the "mud and slush of opinion" and reach Olympus in that messy direction by eating beans and bursting out downward, there is still a "solid bottom everywhere." "If you have built castles in the air," he continues, "your work need not be lost; that is where they should be. Now put the foundations under them." Even the fish in Walden Pond, when they leap after winged food, describe an arch, "an arc of three or four feet in the air, and there is one bright flash where it emerges, and another where it strikes the water; sometimes the whole silvery arc is revealed." Hungry fish, as wholly occupied with the jump as Thoreau, vault out of their lower watery world into the higher one of air. Wisdom, in a word, may come in a flash, and learning is always accompanied by light.

To be sure, arcs are not exactly arches, nor are arches exactly rainbows, but fish and people all trace the same figure. Advancing "confidently in the direction of his dreams," Thoreau tells us that he once "stood in the very abutment of a rainbow's arch, which filled the lower stratum of the atmosphere, tinging the grass and leaves around, and dazzling me as if I looked through colored crystal. It was a lake of rainbow light, in which for a short while, I lived like a dolphin." Leaving the paradise of Baker Farm, Thoreau found himself running "down the hill toward the reddening west, with the rainbow over my shoulder." Like a leaping dolphin, he cannot sustain his airy flight, but he can stay in the air long enough to navigate the Rainbow Bridge of communication, which in the North leads to and from the home of the gods, who sometimes wear blue when they come over to visit us.

On the other side of the rainbow, which abuts the third and integrative side of *Walden*, Thoreau is rightly visited by "a blue-robed man, whose fittest roof is the overarching sky which reflects his serenity." The arching forms of nature, in

157

addition, integrate our minds and the world, when in "Spring" we are "particularly attracted by the arching and sheaf-like top of wool-grass; it brings back the summer to our winter memories, and is among the forms which art loves to copy, and which, in the vegetable kingdom, have the same relation to types already in the mind of man that astronomy has." The cow jumps over the moon, and the highest and most subtle arches support the rafters of the sky, where the circling hawk has a nest "made in the angle of a cloud, woven of the rainbow's trimmings and the sunset sky." Thoreau caps his use of this protean image in a way which applies to the book he has written. "It affords me no satisfaction," he reports, "to commence to spring an arch before I have got a solid foundation."

In this way the arch becomes another kind of barbed *gumphus*, the steely barb of truth which underpins the ethereal equivalences with which *Walden* closes, at first as the bridge over ignorance and then as the act of crossing over. In fact, Thoreau so manages the image that it easily merges into others, just as any figure—as but one of myriad *links* to enlightenment—may be regarded as an arch in function if not in actual form. The arch is the figure the mind executes when it migrates to other climes in clouds. This interchangeability of metaphors, as literary expressions of the mutual identity of all things, anticipates Thoreau's ultimate answer that he "awoke to an answered question, to Nature and daylight." Rightly read, heaven and earth are the same place. When we return from heaven, we rise up to learn again that "Olympus is but the outside of the earth everywhere."

Thoreau is thus able to speak *without* bounds, because he does not limit himself to any particular metaphor. His meaning resides outside language—his is not a giant white fish tale. He engages metaphor itself, and thus the world, as the interface between the mind and heaven, as he weaves another "basket of a delicate texture." In a prophetic anticipation of the string theory of modern physics, each strand ties into yet coincides with every other strand. We may trace these secret threads and catch a moving image of truth in our net of words, because the interrelatedness of the one and the many generates a *unity of equivalences*. The merging of one activity with another may be diagrammed as a multidimensional series of transformations:

> To read *Walden* = to take stock = to enter the right business = to seek life's meaning = to hunt for truth = to migrate = to change = to mature = to etherealize = to wake up = to be alive = to prosper in celestial trade = to read *Walden*....

We may enter *Walden*'s sovereign woods at any point. The "paths which the mind travels" are not one-way streets; and if we follow that path which "rightfully attracts" us and "travel the only path" we can, then "no power can resist" us. Our path may be *to enter the right business* or:

> To seek life's meaning = to grow beans = to cultivate truth = to explore yourself = to harvest truth.

The body becomes a single organ which can, as the mind descends into it, find its way home. Head does become hands and feet, and fingers can see. Every act done well is the same act, so that in *Walden*, if nouns can change places, verbs can assume an iridescent synonymity. Every direction leads to heaven.

> To read well = to dig for truth = to swim for it = to fly for it = to migrate = to get there = to know = to be.

In *Walden* words become instruments of being, as well as saying, so that communication is measured by the extent to which knowing changes into being, as another form of the same activity.

The measure of Thoreau's achievement in helping us, through words, to live this unsayable truth may be viewed in comparison to Emerson's *Nature*, which, though written earlier, stands strangely as a gloss to the later *Walden*. *Nature* is the castle in the air for which *Walden* lays the foundation. The parallel treatment of the intangible value of the land-scape shows Emerson to be the more "scholar-like" of the two. Emerson writes: "There is a property in the horizon which no man has but he whose eye can integrate all its parts, that is, the poet. This is the best part of these men's farms, yet to this their warranty-deed gives no title." Thoreau describes the poet in the same way.

> I have frequently seen a poet withdraw, having enjoyed the most valuable part of a farm, while the crusty farmer supposed that he had got a few wild apples only. Why, the owner does not know it for many years when a poet has put his farm in rhyme, the most admirable kind of invisible fence, has fairly impounded it, milked it, skimmed it, and got all the cream, and left the farmer only the skimmed milk.

Thoreau's Baker Farm version of this withdrawal from the bank of nature shows that he is the poet Emerson names and he himself describes. He tells us that he returned the farm, "but I retained the landscape, and I have since annually carried off what it yielded without a wheelbarrow."

In *Walden* Nature is "not afraid to exhibit herself," and to be "carried off," but only by those who are "in a peculiar sense a part of Nature themselves." Thoreau tasted beans and ate the world. In his *Journal* Emerson reports, "I dreamed ... I ate the world." Thoreau's advice for co-authors is to taste beans and to climb confidently in the direction of our dreams, and to do this "you only need sit still long enough in some attractive spot in the woods that all its inhabitants may exhibit themselves to you by turns." If we set about sitting still and read Thoreau's tropes as "deliberately and reservedly" as he wrote them, we will gain some cheering information from the airy beasts of burden reflected in *Walden*.